THE
ST ANDREWS
O P E N S

THE
ST ANDREWS
OPENS

Bobby Burnet

Historian to the Royal and Ancient Golf Club of St Andrews

Foreword by
Michael Bonallack

SPORTSPRINT PUBLISHING
EDINBURGH

TO BUNTY
The value of a good wife is far above rubies

© John Donald Publishers Ltd 1990

John Donald Publishers Ltd.,
138 St. Stephen Street,
Edinburgh EH3 5AA

ISBN 0 85976 301 3

Design: Keith Kail, Falkirk

Typesetting: Newtext Composition, Glasgow.
Printed and bound in Great Britain by Butler & Tanner Ltd., Frome, Somerset.

FOREWORD

A N OPEN CHAMPIONSHIP AT ST. ANDREWS is totally different to any other. If you are not fortunate enough to have experienced this by actually being there, the next best thing is to read Bobby Burnet's charming accounts of each of the Opens that have been played over the marvellous Old Course.

Every Championship has its own story and the dramatic events of these are beautifully related by Bobby with his undisguised enthusiasm and great love for the game of golf, its players and in particular St. Andrews.

A favourite winter pastime for golfers is to try and compare the great Champions of different eras, an interesting but largely unrewarding exercise. The Champion of his day can only beat those who are competing against him on the same golf course and using the equipment of that time. This book does not set out to make comparisons but it does illustrate that the Old Course poses its own particular problems and that all these great Champions have had to tackle it with the same skill, patience and test of character. No other comparisons are necessary.

No doubt when the 1990 Championship is ended more stories of disaster and triumph wait to be told, but whatever the outcome I am sure that after reading this book one will realise that regardless of modern technology and equipment the character of the Open and indeed the character of golf have not really altered at all, only the cast has changed.

M. F. BONALLACK
Secretary
March 1990

ACKNOWLEDGEMENTS

WHILE I WAS WRITING THIS BOOK I became indebted to many people, some of whom I am bound to have omitted from the following acknowledgements, and for that I must apologise in advance:

The Royal and Ancient Golf Club has allowed me to build up the reference side of what is a comparatively small golf library to a point where there is solid coverage of some kind from 1869 to the present day. In particular I have had access to complete sets of *Golfing Annual*, 1887 to 1910, *Golf*, 1890 to 1899, and *Golf Illustrated* from then until 1914. I could never have finished the book in under a year without two special advantages: the R&A provided a personal photocopier; and my son David compiled a card index to all that vital material, an invaluable source of information which I could then extend later.

Philip Truett, Historian to Walton Heath Golf Club, has supplied most of the original magazines now photocopied and bound, especially *Golfing*, 1913 to 1943, as well as some photographs from his original sources. The Royal Liverpool Golf Club allowed me to have photocopied the first eight volumes of Thomas Owen Potter's Scrapbook, 1869 to 1893; Royal Perth Golfing Society provided similar facilities with their 'Golf Jottings', 1884 to 1894; Royal Eastbourne lent eight volumes of *Golf*; and Bea Auchterlonie has presented a wide range of golf books and magazines, especially *Golf Monthly* almost complete between 1943 and 1976.

For over twenty years now I have been grateful to St. Andrews University for allowing me, as an admitted reader, to use their splendid library facilities, not least their microfilm of early newspapers, and bound copies of later ones. Jim Wilkinson and his bindery staff have bound up many volumes of reference material, both originals and photocopies. I am especially grateful to Peter Adamson, Margaret Smith and Kathleen Macnaughton for processing so many illustrations.

For permission to reproduce black and white illustrations I am indebted to D.C. Thomson & Co. Ltd., Dundee, the Cowie Collection of St. Andrews University and Ian Joy, St. Andrews, and for colour illustrations to Brian Morgan of *Golf Photography International*, Lawrence Levy of *Yours in Sport*, and Ian Joy.

Special thanks are due to Linda Tait for her help throughout in typing each chapter as I completed it, and making alterations and additions there and then through the marvels of word processing. Her help required the generous permission of George Wilson, the Deputy Secretary of the R&A. Kitty Douglas and her staff have been most helpful, especially Pat Ciesla who has done much typing for me over several years.

I am grateful to John Donald Publishers for inviting me to write this book in the first place.

Finally, I extend my warmest thanks to the Secretary, Michael Bonallack, not only for writing his generous Foreword, but for his helpful advice throughout.

BOBBY BURNET,
Royal and Ancient Golf Club of St. Andrews, 1990.

CONTENTS

A MAP OF THE OLD COURSE AT ST. ANDREWS

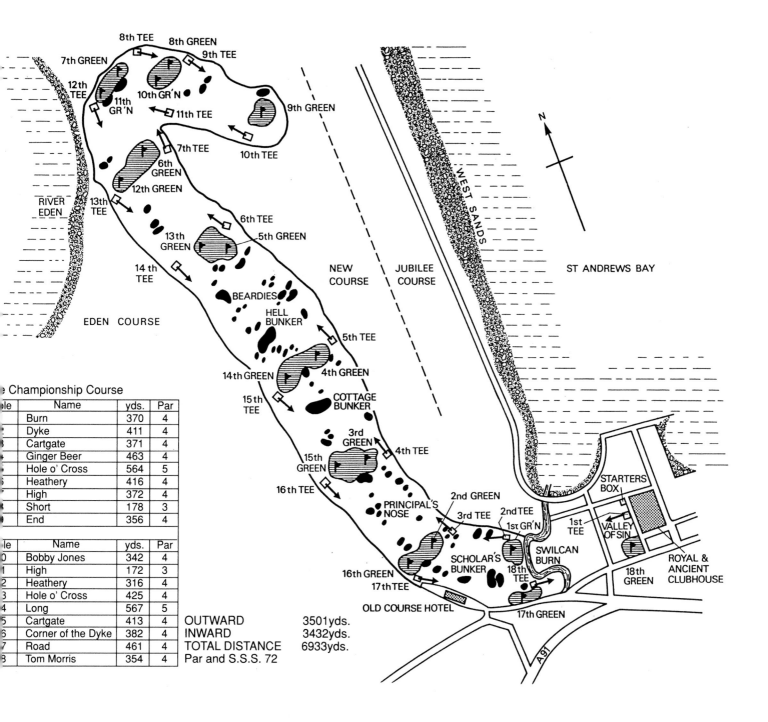

Championship Course

le	Name	yds.	Par
	Burn	370	4
	Dyke	411	4
	Cartgate	371	4
	Ginger Beer	463	4
	Hole o' Cross	564	5
	Heathery	416	4
	High	372	4
	Short	178	3
	End	356	4

le	Name	yds.	Par
0	Bobby Jones	342	4
1	High	172	3
2	Heathery	316	4
3	Hole o' Cross	425	4
4	Long	567	5
5	Cartgate	413	4
6	Corner of the Dyke	382	4
7	Road	461	4
8	Tom Morris	354	4

OUTWARD   3501yds.
INWARD   3432yds.
TOTAL DISTANCE   6933yds.
Par and S.S.S. 72

Crowds on the Old Course, 1950s. The St. Andrews skyline beyond.

CHAPTER 1

A BRIEF ACCOUNT OF GOLF HISTORY

*L*IKE *NATURE, HISTORY ABHORS A VACUUM;* events must be set in their contexts if they are to be of real interest. With that in mind, a brief account of golf history should be helpful before discussing the seeds of the Open Championship as started by Prestwick Golf Club in 1860.

Nobody knows exactly where or when golf started up first. It could have been at Aberdeen, Montrose, St. Andrews, Carnoustie or Leith. Leith seems the most likely because that was near the capital and it would be easier to get around. But there are many people who make claims for different places, always on the east coast of Scotland. There were other games like Jeu de Mail, the game with a mallet, which is described in the history of croquet; of course, you were liable to be hitting the ball through a hoop in that case. Then there was Dutch Kolf and there you might be hitting the ball against a door, a pillar, a post or even along a frozen river. But, it did not involve putting into a hole which is the distinguishing feature of golf. If in fact you were playing one version of Dutch Kolf, a back-handed game on ice, and you hit the ball into a hole you would lose your ball every time! The Dutch make all kinds of claims about their game as being the first golf and there has been much argument about it. They talk about the derivation of the word 'tee', claiming that the Scots 'tee' derives from 'tuitje', meaning a heap of sand. However, in the earliest written Rules in 1744 the second Rule says: 'Your tee must be upon the ground' and since you cannot place a heap of sand in the air, Scots 'tee' has really nothing to do with Dutch 'tuitje'. Surely if we had imported our 'golf,' 'gowf' or 'goff' from Holland it would have been called 'Kolf'?

Golf as we know it started up on the east coast of Scotland on the Links land: that is, the non-arable ground with beautiful undulating turf, sand never very far down; and, with the wind changing all the time, you would seldom play the same golf course twice. In various coastal areas it was the Laird, the local Landlord, who allowed, in a lovely phrase, 'a servitude of golf'. The citizens were entitled to play golf in that area 'from time immemorial'. One of the early ideas about how golf originated came from Sir Walter Simpson about 1890 in his *Art of Golf*. His idea was that perhaps a shepherd would be getting bored and might turn his crook round, take a stone and knock it along. Then perhaps he would find it more interesting if he made a hole in the ground and knocked the stone into the hole. It is not all that fanciful because, you see, sheep were grazing on this Links land, keeping the course playable before mowing machines were invented. I mentioned this theory to a Rotary Club, and afterwards a big farmer came up and said, 'Don't be so daft. What shepherd would damage his crook by hitting stones? He might well have used dried sheep-dung'.

Women were allowed to bleach clothes on the edge of the golf course, so that in the 1842

Jeu de Mail, the game with a mallet. From Lauthier, *Nouveaux Règles pour le Jeu de Mail* (1717).

Rules it said: 'When a ball lies on clothes, or within a club-length of a washing tub, the clothes may be drawn from under the ball, and the tub may be removed'. A South Korean film crew came to St. Andrews to make an informative programme for tourists now that people under 50 are being allowed to leave the country. The interpreter asked me to tell him in a few words the history of golf and I suggested that the origin might have been produced by Simpson's shepherd. Very soon, at the front of the Clubhouse, I was talking to a South Korean presenter, a very beautiful young girl, who said, 'You tell me the history of golf, please'. For about 45 seconds I talked about shepherds and crooks, waving arms wildly or making putting movements – and that was the history of golf!

It was in 1457 that James II of Scotland introduced a statute 'utterly crying down' golf and football because they were getting in the way of archery. The defence of the Realm was declining, and we were losing battles against the English, a dreadful situation. It is commonly thought that the 1457 Statute was the first of its kind and argued a special foresight and patriotism on the part of Scotland. But here, as in so much else, the French were first in the field. In 1319 they had banned all games of ball, to protect archery; and in 1337 the English passed a similar law, with a death penalty for non-observance. But there had been golf on the

Dutch Kolf being played within a court (1792).

VERHANDELING

OVER DE OORSPRONG VAN HET

KOLVEN,

Onderwys in de Manier hoe het Spel gefpeelt word, en Ordonnantie op het Kolven. De Nuttigheid van dit Spel boven anderen fpeelen aangepreezen. Regifter der Spreekwoorden, in het Nederduitsch en Fransch. En eindelyk een Naamwyzer der Kolfbaanen binnen en buiten Amfterdam, als ook in verfcheide andere Steden en Dorpen.

Opgeftelt tot vermaak der Liefhebbers.

DE TWEEDE VERBETERDE DRUK.

Te AMSTERDAM,
By JAN ROOS, EN
GERBRAND ROOS,
Boekverkoopers.
MDCCXCII.

Dutch clubmaker's shop c. 1780.

ZINSPEELING op den KOLVENMAAKER.

Wie 't Kolven 't eerft heeft uitgevonden
Is niet bekend op vafte gronden;
  Miffchien een fchrandre Jongen wel;
  Want eertyds was het Kinderfpel.
Maar 't is meer dan een Eeuw geleeden,
Toen 't reeds bedaagde Lieden deeden,
  Tot men vervolgens verder kwam,
  Het Kind de Klik en 't Klootje ontnam
En vlak gevlyde baanen maakte,
Waarin men ftraks aan 't Kolven raakte
  Om tot het een en ander end,
  Gelyk 't een ieder is bekend,
Den Bal de Stukken te doen treffen,
Die zich ter beider eind verheffen,
  Omringd van Schutting en Rabat,
  Voor elk die fmaak in 't Kolven had.
Dit deed het Kolvenmaaken bloeijen;
De Bal'en raakten ook aan 't groeijen,
  Tot zesponds Kogels groote op 't minft
  Dit geeft den Kolvenmaaker winft.

Elk werkt om aan de koft te raaken;
Zo doen wy ook met Kolvenmaaken.
Men rolt den Bal niet door de baan,
Maar moet 'er met de Kolf op flaan.

Golf (?), from a fourteenth-century Flemish manuscript book of prayer.

Links land for at least a century before 1457, so we are talking about 1300-1350. The best records really of golf in those times and onwards are found in the Kirk Session Minutes. For instance, in St. Andrews in 1599 the Kirk Session decreed that 'who so is found golfing during the time of divine service shall for the first offence pay ten shillings, twenty shillings for the second, for the third be placed on the repentance pillar and for the fourth be deprived of office' – in other words, be excommunicated. The fines were not so large as it might seem because the Scots pound was worth only a small fraction of the English one; but excommunication was a terrible punishment when hell fire was a very real concept in many Elizabethan minds.

'Prophaning' the Lord's Sabbath. From Clark's *Golf* (1875).

King James VI and I, an early
devotee of golf.

Browning begins his excellent *History of Golf* (1955) with a chapter entitled 'Why Golf is Royal and Ancient', and points out that 'During nearly two hundred years from the Peace of Glasgow in 1502 to the Revolution of 1688, every reigning monarch of the Stuart line – two kings and one queen of Scotland, four kings of the United Kingdom – was a golfer.' In just over five pages, Browning gives a fine summary of Royal Stuart golf; what a pity it is that his book now costs over £100 – if a copy becomes available. He refers to:

> one of the charges brought against . . . the beautiful and ill-fated Mary, Queen of Scots . . . that within a few days of the murder of her husband, Darnley, she had been seen 'playing golf and pall-mall in the fields beside Seton'.

He added:

> The monarch whose example did most for golf, however, was James IV's great grandson,

5

Enthusiasts of 1896 . . . golf by moonlight.

James VI. When he succeeded to the English throne as James I he took his clubs with him ...

Two pieces of information not recorded by Browning may be of interest. In 'Wormcasts' in *Golf Illustrated*, 10th December, 1909, the last item is: 'Mary, Queen of Scots, once played a match at golf at Seton against Lady Mary Seton; the latter on winning was presented with the famous "Mary Seton" necklace, which was bought by Lord Glenesk in 1894 for £365.' Then, in a letter from Thomas Chapman to *Golf*, February 16, 1894, he says:

> SIR, – In Chalmers's 'Picture of Scotland' (Vol. II., p. 332. Edinburgh. 1827) there is a notice of the Old Tower of Alloa. Dr. Chambers, in the notice, says:– 'In it James VI and his eldest son, Henry, were successively educated, under the care of the Mar family'. The cradle of the former and his little nursery-chair, besides Prince Henry's golfs, were preserved in the Tower till a recent period, when they fell into the possession of Lady Frances Erskine, daughter of the late venerable Earl of Mar, who, we understand, now preserves them, with the care and veneration due to such valuable heirlooms, in her house near Edinburgh.
>
> 'The cradle and the chair are still the property of the Earl of Mar and Kellie, and both are engraved in a superb volume, 'The Royal House of Stuart, drawn by William Gibb, R.S.A.,' Plates 20 and 21, and are in Alloa House. No record seems to exist, however, of 'Prince Henry's golfs,' and, being desirous to trace, if it were possible, these relics of ancient Golf, I applied through a friend to the Earl of Mar and Kellie, who replies: 'I remember hearing my father talk of James VI's Golf stick being at Alloa; but I never saw it, and fear it is not there now'.

I think it is worth discussing the place of the Royal & Ancient Golf Club in the hierarchy of the Golf Clubs. That was always established by the purchase of the Silver Club, in this case by the Society of St. Andrews Golfers in 1754. These eighteenth-century Clubs would have a competition, the winner became Captain for the ensuing year, and attached a silver ball to the club with his name and the date on it. That was cast-iron evidence of when a particular Golf Club was formed. It could happen that the Captain was very young. In the case of Horace Hutchinson, at Westward Ho! he was only sixteen when he won. As he was a very clever fellow he chaired the meetings and acted as Captain, even although he was still in his 'teens. But before outlining the main hierarchy it is as well to discuss Royal Blackheath and Royal Burgess as they both claim to be older than they are. Royal Blackheath always has been entered in the *Golfer's Handbook* as 'instituted traditionally in 1608'; but when they called in Henderson and Stirk to write a book about Royal Blackheath, they could not produce any evidence before 1766 when they had their first Silver Club. Without some concrete evidence you cannot really uphold a reputation for being there since 1608. State Papers during James VI and I's reign from 1603 on give plenty of space to his hunting activities, and many of his letters are extant – but there is never a reference to golf at Blackheath, with or without a golfing society. The other Club, the Royal Burgess, celebrated two hundred and fifty years, as if instituted in 1735, in 1985 and brought out a brochure and all the rest; but they have no evidence of their existence before the 1770s. If we dismiss these two very tenuous claims the oldest Club is, in fact, the Gentleman Golfers at Leith. They later became the Honourable Company of Edinburgh Golfers and they were instituted in 1744. When the Society of St. Andrews Golfers, later the Royal & Ancient, was instituted in 1754 they looked around for other Clubs that they could invite to compete for their Silver Club and made contact with the Gentleman Golfers at Leith. If the Royal Burgess had been instituted almost twenty years before that, surely they would have been called in? But they were not. Then the third Club would be Bruntsfield Links Golfing Society in 1761. The link between golf and Freemasonry from about 1766 onwards has been well established by Henderson and Stirk in their *Royal Blackheath*, but there is no evidence that the Gentlemen Golfers (1744) and the Society of St. Andrews Golfers (1754) were other than formed for golf. Indeed, the R&A has a minute book from 1766 running concurrently with their 1754 to 1800 one, but indicating the social side of the Club. There were other eighteenth-century Clubs: the Glasgow Golf Club (1886) have 'Reconstituted in 1870' on their notepaper; there are also Aberdeen, Crail, Musselburgh, and the last one in the eighteenth century would be Burntisland Golf House Club, instituted in 1797.

Golf, 1858-style, from *Chambers' Journal.* Note cheesecutter caps.

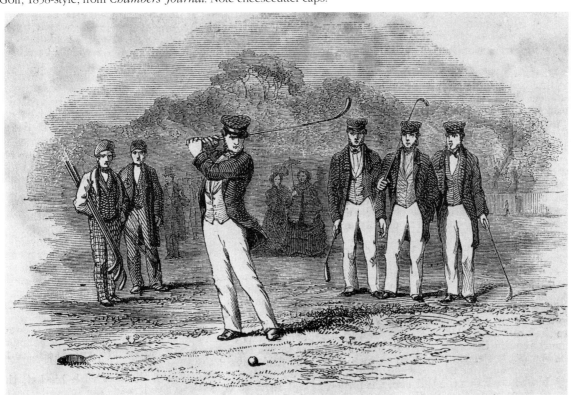

Now, what changes were there in the Old Course since the eighteenth century? If you were looking out at the Old Course, what difference would you see from today? Originally there were twenty-two holes on the Old Course, in 1754, and then in 1764 that was cut back to eighteen holes, nine out and nine back, playing to the same hole on the green each time. Presumably the extra holes, the other two holes, must have been behind the present Clubhouse and starting near the Cathedral; no holes could have been omitted at the far end of the course, the 'loop'. In those days you would have seen that they actually played it left-handed, going first of all to the seventeenth green, with the road bunker coming in in a totally different way and with a great long narrow strip of green, then the road behind. So your second shot – or maybe your third shot – of the morning would present the problem of stopping on the green. The other difference would be that where nowadays there is a certain amount of gorse (whin), there were masses of whin or gorse in the old days and you would find yourself in there if you left the fairway. The greens were very small, with only one pin on each, and homeward-coming players had the right of way. It was about 1830 before someone had the brilliant idea of enlarging the greens and putting two pins on them – and, of course, play speeded up enormously.

The seven great, wide grazing areas for the sheep were in no way landscaped but became these seven huge double greens. As for the bunkers, people reckoned that in a storm the sheep would huddle in a hollow, the sand was not very far down, and so they would break through the crust and a rough bunker would be formed. We have an 1821 map, in fact, of the Old Course giving the distances in miles, furlongs and yards, obviously exactly the same out and back. It comes to a total of 6,388 yards, exactly the same length the Old Course is today if you discount the Championship tees which add on about 500 yards. In the 1890s and before, there were, in fact, different records for playing the Course left-handed and right-handed. Willie Auchterlonie, the 1893 Open Champion, held the record for the left-handed course in that year with a 71.

The earliest Rules, in 1744, were the Gentleman Golfers at Leith's and in 1754 the Society of St. Andrews Golfers'. There were only thirteen Rules originally, very few compared to the large book that we have today; but it is rather like Income Tax: there has to be legislation for a very tiny minority who cheat, and everyone else has to conform. Of these thirteen Rules I would like to pick out one or two that seem to me to be more interesting. First of all there is this matter of teeing the ball. After a while, certainly by the mid-nineteenth century, you did actually make a heap of sand, and put the ball on it for driving off, teeing up quite close to the hole. You extracted sand from the hole to tee up, and after a large number of people had done so you had a great deal of trouble retrieving your ball because you would have to put your arm a long way down so as to get at it. Driving from so close to the hole – 'within a club length of the hole' – must have made the putting extremely difficult. Rule 4 says you are not to remove 'stones, *bones* or any break-club . . .'. *The Scotsman* reported in December 1900:

> In the old times of plague or pest the victims were buried 'en masse' on the links both of
> Musselburgh and *Leith* (where the Gentlemen Golfers played). In the first Rules you were
> never told you must play the ball as it lies; but in fact the thirteenth Rule, the last Rule,
> specified exactly that: 'Neither trench, ditch or dyke . . . shall be accounted a hazard'.

So you had to play the ball where it lay, and it meant that all kinds of very unusual clubs were devised just for extracting the ball from bad lies.

Competitors in the 1857 Grand National Inter-Club Tournament, pictured outside the R&A Clubhouse.

There can be no doubt that as soon as golfers and fellow club members began to bet on the outcome of a match, handicapping had to follow. We still have bet books today showing the very large sums which were involved. They would be playing for a guinea or two guineas in the eighteenth century and that would be far beyond the pocket of any except the gentry. The odds given might be 'one more', a stroke a hole, 'two more', two strokes a hole, or a 'half of one', half a stroke a hole – and so on. Members' bets went into the bet book, and an enormous amount of betting went on, just as it happens at a racetrack nowadays.

Writing in 1896, Horatio Ross gave an eye-witness account of 'The most Remarkable Golf Match ever played':

Lord Kennedy and the late Mr Cruikshank of Langley Park were good players and had frequent matches for large sums of money; but the most remarkable match ever played by them came off during the Montrose race week many years since. At the race ordinary [eating house] they got up a match of three holes for £500 each hole, and agreed to play it then and there. It was about 10 or 10.30 p.m. and quite dark. No light was allowed, except one lantern placed on the hole, and another carried by the attendant of the player, in order that they might ascertain to whom the ball struck belonged . . . Boys were placed along the course who were quite accustomed to the game, to listen to the flight of the balls, and to run to the spot where a ball struck and rested . . . ; it was won, I know, by only one hole . . .

It was in about 1850 that the single most important event in all golf history took place: the arrival of the gutta percha (solid rubber) ball. Until then the feather ball had reigned supreme for centuries but it had enormous drawbacks: it was very expensive; by an exhausting process a man could make only three in a day; and on wet days the seams burst very easily. Using a mould, gutta percha balls could be turned out at the rate of a hundred a day – and the cost instead of 3/- to 5/- was only 6d to 1/-. Suddenly golf came within the financial range of the Scottish working man. It could make little impact on his English counterpart; the Blackheath Club was small and exclusive, and the Old Manchester, the other English Club, instituted in 1818, had only twelve members. The third English Club, Westward Ho!, did not arrive until 1864. In Scotland, however, there were about twenty Clubs by 1850, and by 1860 there were over thirty.

Finally, one of the biggest misconceptions about early golf and St. Andrews is that the Open Championship was the first real Championship, in 1860. If you look at the *Shell International Golf Encyclopedia* you will find that it says there was an Inter-Club tournament in 1857 and it was played at Prestwick. In fact, there were three Grand National tournaments, in 1857, 1858 and 1859, and they were all contested on St. Andrews Links. They were really the first Scottish Amateur Championships because the English were not involved. It was very misleading that the first tournament in 1857, the Inter-Club tournament, was won by Blackheath; for the two men representing Blackheath were very much Scots: Captain John Campbell Stewart of Fasnacloich, and George Glennie from Aberdeen. How Scottish Glennie was, can

Mr George Glennie, by his partner, Thomas Hodge, the club artist.

be deduced from the story about his having played a match as a foursome partner with Thomas Hodge, the Club Artist. Glennie put Hodge into the Swilcan Burn, the ball was a floater; Hodge got out his niblick, went into the Burn and played the ball out right beside the hole. Glennie said – I'm sure with a twinkle in his eye – 'it's no gowf, jist monkey tricks!' Again in 1858 the first real knockout tournament took place, Amateur, and that was won by Robert Chambers of the publishing firm, after a great battle.

CHAPTER 2

THE SEEDS OF THE OPEN CHAMPIONSHIP

*T*HERE IS NO DOUBT AT ALL THAT PRESTWICK GOLF CLUB had the honour of instituting the Open Championship, and that they ran it entirely by themselves between 1860 and 1872, with a gap in 1871 when they were without a trophy to present. (Young Tom Morris had made it his property by winning the Championship Belt three times running between 1868 and 1870.)

What very few realise is that Prestwick Golf Club was not instituted until 1851; and although Shaw in his *History* (1938) claims that golf had been played on Prestwick links for centuries, the evidence does not support him:

> Coming to the forties of the nineteenth century, the Earl of Eglinton with a party would travel from Eglinton Castle to Prestwick for a game – the railway was opened in 1843 and his lordship had the privilege of stopping any train by which he wanted to travel – laying out a course for themselves and cutting their own putting holes. Of course there were no greens then as now. The custom was just to scutch away the long grass immediately round the hole, the green being only a few feet in diameter.

(William Galbraith, *Prestwick St Nicholas Golf Club*, page 4)

On the other hand the Royal and Ancient Golf Club had been in existence since 1754 and as early as 1819 had run a competition exactly similar to the Prestwick Opens: for the professionals – the clubmakers, ballmakers and caddies – on the second day of the Autumn Meeting. In 1819 the R&A Minutes mention the 'in-puts', money subscribed by the Members for professional competition. Perhaps the earliest reference to professional golfers is found in a cutting from the *Fifeshire Journal* in 1835, the earliest newspaper report in Allan Robertson's Golf Album, one of the R&A's treasures. We are told that in September 1835,

> On Thursday a match was played betwixt the two St Andrews Pieries (i.e. Piries) and Robert Oliphant, younger of Rossie, and Thomas Alexander, famed on the Burntisland Links; and after playing on the course two rounds, the Pieries gained by seven holes; they are undoubtedly the first players in Scotland.

The report on the Autumn Meeting dated October 11th 1838 describes how on the Wednesday 'The golf club medal' had been won by Mr Robert Haig, Seggie, at 112 strokes, with four others on 114. 'The day was bright and beautiful.' On the Thursday the scores were decidedly professional when the 'inputs (a sweepstakes)' were played for: 'The candidates played for the in-puts which were won by Mr Geddes of Musselburgh at 93 strokes – Alex Pirie came in at 97. This was reckoned very crack playing.'

The following year there is the first mention of Allan Robertson in any report when, on

JAMES WILSON   BOB ANDREW.   WILLIE DUNN.   WILLIE PARK.   ALLAN ROBERTSON.   TOM MORRIS.   BOB KIRK.
(CLUBMAKER).   ("THE ROOK").   D. ANDERSON ("DAW").

Golfing scene c. 1854-5.

17th October, 1839 it says: 'The in-puts were carried by Allan Robertson, St. Andrews.'

The next piece of information dated October 20th 1842 is very important indeed. At the very end of the account of the Autumn Meeting there are details of the contest for the in-puts, won by Tom Morris when he himself was still 'Thomas Morris junior'. (Allan was then 27 and Tom 21): 'On Friday morning the in-puts (a sweepstakes [sic]) were played for by the caddies. These were gained by Thomas Morris junior who holed the Links at 92 strokes, Thomas Morris senior at 99; and Alexander Herd at 103'. Allan Robertson was 'prohibited by his brethren from competing for these stakes on account of his superior play, it being their impression that they would have no chance in any contest in which Allan took part'. This is the only really concrete evidence of how good Allan was in his absolute prime.

Now James Ogilvy Fairlie of Coodham near Prestwick, was the most famous amateur golfer of his day, had become a member of the R&A in 1838, the year when the competition for the 'in-puts' was first reported, and was its Captain in 1850, the year before Prestwick Golf Club was instituted. While in office in the following May 1851 he arranged that Tom Morris and his family – young Tom was only a baby – moved to Prestwick. It was reported like this: 'Tom departs from St. Andrews for Ayrshire in the end of this month, to a place in the vicinity of Ayr, called Prestwick, where they have links, and upon which Tom will likely soon astonish the natives of those parts: he will no doubt reign supreme as a golfer.' Tom's deadly rival from the mid-1850s was Willie Park Senior of Musselburgh; and one main factor in persuading Prestwick to initiate the Open Championship in 1860 was the prospect of exciting clashes

Colonel James O. Fairlie of Coodham, as Captain of the R&A, 1850. From the Captains Book at the R&A.

between Morris and Park. Fairlie was the prime mover in all this. It was his suggestion on 30th May, 1860 that 'a private subscription should be opened with a view to procure a Medal for professionals to be competed for under regulations submitted to the meeting'. As Browning put it: 'The sum of five guineas was subscribed right away in the room, but hope of support from other Clubs was not realized and in the end the Prestwick Club took the whole responsibility on its own shoulders.' (The Belt was substituted for the proposed medal.)

Clearly, Colonel Fairlie was very often at the R&A's Autumn Meeting between 1838 when he became a Member and 1860 when he suggested procuring 'a Medal for Professionals'. But can it be established that he was actually present on an occasion when the professionals are known to have been playing for the 'in-puts' on the second day of the Meeting? Captain Fairlie, as he then was, is not named in the *Fifeshire Journal*'s reports in 1838 and 1839; he would have needed to play very well to receive a mention. Fortunately, he did just that in 1842: in playing for King William IV's Medal and the Club Gold Medal 'Mr Robert Haig and Captain Fairlie' were third equal 'next in order to the Major (Playfair) each having taken 109 strokes'. Fairlie also attended the Ball on that Thursday, and the following morning 'Tom Morris Junior' won the "in-puts" as already mentioned, Allan Robertson having been 'prohibited by his brethren from competing'.

It does seem quite possible, then, that Colonel Fairlie, long before 1860, had seen at St. Andrews the seeds of the Open Championship.

CHAPTER 3

THE EARLY PRESTWICK
OPENS: 1860-1872

A *WEST OF SCOTLAND REPORT* of Prestwick's Autumn Meeting in 1860 had, under the heading THE CHALLENGE BELT:

'Recognising the desirability of providing some annual test to gauge the comparative merits of professional golfers, the Prestwick Club, with characteristic enthusiasm and liberality, lately subscribed for a Challenge Belt, open for competition in the three kingdoms. The Trophy, which consists of red morocco, is an exquisite piece of workmanship, richly ornamented with various devices in silver, and cost, we believe, twenty-five guineas. But apart from its intrinsic value . . . its custody for the first year at least fired the ambition of

A calotype of Robert Chambers winning the 1858 Golf Tournament at St. Andrews. *Evening Telegraph*, Dundee.

below
Old Tom Morris, faithful caddy to Col. J. O. Fairlie of Coodham.

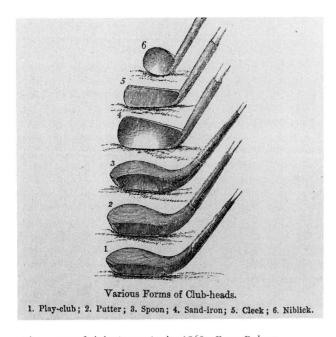

Various Forms of Club-heads.
1. Play-club; 2. Putter; 3. Spoon; 4. Sand-iron; 5. Cleek; 6. Niblick.

The range of clubs in use in the 1860s. From Robert Chambers Jr., *A Few Rambling Remarks* . . . (1862).

the crack men of the best greens in the empire. There was a large number of aspirants whose praise was on all the links in the country: and despite the unpropitious weather, a great concourse of the patrons of the ancient game was attracted to Prestwick to witness a contest which had excited an interest unprecedented in golfing circles. Eight celebrities preferred their claims to the honour, and were paired off as follows:-

1. Thomas Morris, Prestwick Golf Club, and Robert Andrew, Perth.
2. William Park, Musselburgh, and Alexander Smith, Bruntsfield, Edinburgh.
3. Wm. Steel, Bruntsfield, and Charles Hunter, St. Nicholas Club, Prestwick.
4. George Daniel Brown, Blackheath, and Andrew Strath, St. Andrews.

Perhaps it is unfair to mention that one 'celebrity', William Steel, Bruntsfield, took 232 for the 36 holes, sixteen over sixes! The contest was fought out between the 'Prestwick and Musselburgh champions'; Tom Morris was expected to beat Willie Park over Prestwick, but Park won by two shots. Tom was often in sand. As the report put it:

> . . . the most veteran frequenters of the links will admit that in all their experience of Morris they never saw him come to grief so often, because it is well known that the battle of Bunker's Hill is an engagement which he has very seldom to fight.

In 1861 there was a much stronger entry, including the Dunn brothers, but this time Tom won by four shots from Willie Park. Park was two strokes up after two rounds, 24 holes, but the report mentions with great glee a disastrous hole by Park which swung the whole contest:

> In approaching the second hole of the final round, however, a daring attempt to "cross the Alps" in two brought Park's ball into one of the worst hazards on the green and cost him three strokes – by no means the first time he has been severely punished for similar avarice and temerity.

The leading Amateurs including Colonel Fairlie and Captain Stewart of Fasnacloich, had competed in 1861; but Fairlie, who made the best amateur return, was 21 shots behind the winner – over 36 holes.

J. McBain in his 1903 articles on the Golf Championship Belt Contests had this to say about 1862:

> The 1862 Championship was held on September 10th. From the smallness of the field which turned up on this occasion one would be apt to conclude that interest in the event was beginning to wane among both professionals and amateurs. So to a certain extent it was. The prowess of the champion and ex-champion was so predominant that very few cared to oppose them. The disastrous experience of the two Dunns at the previous Championship, the acknowledged rivals of Morris and Park, did not encourage them to compete again for some years, and the others apparently did not think the game worth the candle. The only professionals present in addition to the two champions, were W. Dow of Musselburgh and Charlie Hunter, the Prestwick professional. The leading amateurs had made such a poor show that none of them ventured again to expose their weaknesses at this meeting. Four amateurs, all local men, took their place. Tom Morris was in good form, and fairly ran away from Park, who was the reverse. The champion gained seven strokes on Park in the first round, was eleven up on the completion of the second round, and at the conclusion of the third round won by thirteen strokes over Park.

McBain discussed the prize-money in 1863:

> . . . in the minutes of Prestwick's 1863 autumn meeting we find it reported that The Club offered the following prizes to be competed for in the game for the champion belt – viz, to the second a prize of five pounds, to the third a prize of three pounds, and to the fourth a prize of two pounds . . . No money, it will be noticed, was offered to the champion.

On the following day the fourth championship meeting took place. The weather was thoroughly unfavourable, and this was reflected in the scoring. Park took 168 and Morris 170, and Tom thus missed by three strokes winning the belt outright.

More money was contributed for the ensuing Championship in 1864. The amount was increased to £15, and the champion was included, and awarded the first-place money in addition to the belt. The meeting intimated to the various professionals that the following prizes would be given, viz: To the winner of the belt £6, to the second £5, to the third £3, to the fourth £1. On summing up the cards it was found that Tom Morris was the winner of the belt and £6, in 167, A. Strath (St. Andrews) being second at 169, Robert Andrew third at 175, and Willie Park fourth at 177.

It was in 1864 that Tom Morris returned to St. Andrews. Alexander Herd had resigned the custody of St. Andrews Links and the Committee were authorised to appoint a custodian 'at a salary considerably larger than that hitherto given'. We know that just seven years earlier W. Alexander and A. Herd had received a joint £6 'for keeping the golf course during past year'. The increase in salary certainly was considerable, as an R&A Minute dated 4th May, 1864 shows:

> Major Boothby moved that Thos. Morris of Prestwick formerly of St. Andrews be brought here as a professional golfer . . . on the understanding that he shall have entire charge of the golf course and be responsible for it being kept in proper order, and that he shall be the servant of the Club under the direction and control of the Committee in charge of the green . . .

The sum of £50 per annum was voted for payment of Tom's salary, and £20 for the upkeep of the links. In January 1865 this was stated more fully, granting him one man's labour for two days a week when heavy work such as carting was to be done.

In 1865 Young Tom, aged fourteen, competed for the Belt for the first time; but as he retired after 24 of the 36 holes, the fact is omitted in the histories. His father, now 44, defended the championship. The winner was Andrew Strath who is given as playing out of St. Andrews in several main histories and encyclopedias: but he had in fact succeeded Tom Morris as Custodian of Prestwick Links in 1864, and this gave him a chance to acquire some of the local knowledge built up by the Morrises during their years in Prestwick from 1851 on. Tom was very badly out of form, finishing fourteen behind Strath, and in fact Young Tom was a shot better than his father when he decided to give up!

In 1866, the brothers Park, Willie and David, came first and second respectively – a triumph for Musselburgh. The Morrises were decidedly off form. The expense involved in reaching Prestwick from the East coast was considerable, and some early sponsorship resulted.

Old and Young Tom Morris c. 1874.

The *Scotsman* reported:

> Hitherto, on account of the great distance, thereby involving great expense, the number of competitors at Prestwick has been very small. In order to meet this difficulty a subscription list was drawn up, and money sufficient to defray the expenses of three of the best players was raised among the gentlemen golfers of Musselburgh and Edinburgh.

In 1867, Tom Morris won for the fourth and last time, by two shots from his old rival Willie Park. Andrew Strath was two strokes further back. The 1865 Champion had a tragically short career for by Autumn 1868 he was dead. Young Tom had taken a huge 187 the previous year and this time was five shots behind his father. There was no hint of how well he would play during the next three years in winning the Belt outright.

As the scoring was very high in 1867, the following from *Golf Illustrated* in 1900 may well be relevant:

> Mr J.O. Fairlie . . . tells me he has a driving putter of his father's which Old Tom always says won for him the Champion Belt at Prestwick on a very windy day. Tom came to the Colonel as he arrived from Coodham and asked to borrow the driving putter. Willie Park arrived soon afterwards with the same request – but he was too late.

As the two main reference books give a totally garbled version of the results when Young Tom won in 1868 and 1869, it will be as well to give the details of the first six in each, as provided in MacArthur's *Golfer's Annual* for 1869-1870, and also the 1870 results:

1868

1.	T. Morris jun.	51	54	49	=	154
2.	T. Morris sen.	54	50	53	=	157
3.	Robert Andrew	53	54	52	=	159
4.	W. Park	58	50	54	=	162
5.	R. Ferguson	57	54	54	=	165
6.	T. Dunn	59	54	54	=	167

1869

1.	T. Morris jun.	50	55	52	=	157
2.	Bob Kirk	53	58	57	=	168
3.	D. Strath	53	56	60	=	169
4.	J. Anderson	60	56	57	=	173
5.	W. Doleman	60	56	59	=	175
6.	T. Morris sen.	56	62	58	=	176

1870

1.	T. Morris jun.	47	51	51	=	149
2.	D. Strath	54	49	58	=	161
3.	R. Kirk	52	52	57	=	161
4.	T. Morris	56	52	54	=	162
5.	W. Doleman	57	54	58	=	169
6.	W. Park	60	55	58	=	173

What stands out is that Young Tom was a staggering total of 26 shots better than the runners-up in these three Challenge Belt contests. McBain's comments on this performance have two interesting features: he discusses one particular shot in 1869, and later the difficulties presented by Prestwick links as they applied to Young Tom:

> The 1869 championship . . . was attended by very favourable conditions . . . Young Tom Morris was again the victor . . . A lucky tee shot to the station, or eighth hole, contributed to the 50 in the first round, for he holed the shot . . . In 1870 . . . one can easily picture to oneself the astonishment of the spectators . . . when . . . he . . . completed the first round of twelve holes in 47, one under fours. It is only when we consider the conditions under which it was made that the superlative merit of the performance becomes fully apparent. Prestwick was then a very long course, being two miles 230 yards for the twelve holes: it was beset with hazards, was not nearly so fine as it is today, and the smoothness of the greens not at all to be compared with the state they are now kept in . . . In paying Young Tommy so high a compliment, it must not be forgotten that he was playing over what was virtually his own green. He had learned to play golf over the links. When quite a child he had come to Prestwick along with his father, who had been professional and green-keeper to the Prestwick Golf Club for thirteen years, and the boy had learned all his golf there. He was so familiar with the round that he could almost have played it blind-folded.

After the blank year in 1871, following Young Tom Morris's outright winning of the Belt in 1870, Prestwick decided to invite the Royal and Ancient and the Honourable Company of Edinburgh Golfers (then at Musselburgh near Edinburgh) to join in putting up a new silver Trophy, the 'Golf Champion Trophy' as the famous claret jug is inscribed. But when Young Tom won for the fourth consecutive time the Trophy did not exist. John Bowles, an expert on sporting trophies, has discovered that the hallmark on the Trophy is the Date Letter for 1873/74. Bowles concluded 'that after final agreement was reached the new Trophy could not be made in time for the 1872 event, that it was a full year before it was produced, that the medal served in part as a temporary presentation and that the Trophy was finally completed late in 1873 and the first engraved record back-dated to 1872.'

The medal is not of solid gold as in later years but in gold-plated base metal. This led Willie Park Jnr, the Champion Golfer in 1887 and 1889, to state quite bluntly that anything other than gold was inadequate as a reward for such a victory. By 1893 – because the Royal and Ancient has Willie Auchterlonie's 'Open' medal – solid gold was used.

It is interesting that the inscription on Young Tom's 1872 Medal is 'Golf Champion Trophy' so that anyone reading the contemporary accounts of that Open Championship would assume that he received the non-existent claret jug.

CHAPTER 4

...AND SO TO ST. ANDREWS: TOM KIDD, 1873

WHENEVER THE FIRST OPEN CHAMPIONSHIP at St. Andrews in 1873 is mentioned, the winner, Tom Kidd, is described as having taken the highest number of strokes for the 36 holes required by anyone between then and 1892 at Muirfield when 72 holes became the set number. That is true – but the suggestion that conditions were perfect on that fourth of October, 1873, which appears in several histories, is far wide of the mark.

In Mortimer and Pignon's *Story of the Open Championship: 1860-1950*, for instance, they say: 'But the championship of 1873 was perhaps the most mysterious of the whole series, and why anyone was allowed "to get away with it" with so high a score has never been explained. Yet the scoring ruled high on that day and it cannot be blamed on the weather; for we happen to know that the weather was perfect for golfing purposes.'

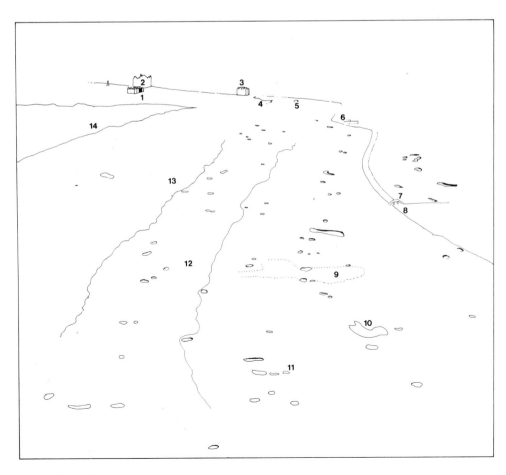

The St. Andrews setting: Aerial view of the Old Course during the 1957 Open. The railway is still there, and the Old Course Hotel has yet to be built. 1: The R&A. 2: Former Grand Hotel, perhaps built out of spite by a spurned applicant for membership of the R&A. 3: Rusack's Hotel. 4: Swilcan Burn. 5: Road Bunker at 17th. 6: Black Sheds, 17th tee. 7: Former bridge from Eden to Old Course. 8: Railway line from which Braid played in 1905. 9: 4th & 14th greens. 10: Hell Bunker. 11: Cruel, deep bunkers at the 5th; Braid and Jones could get on the green in two. 12: New Course. 13: Jubilee Course. 14: West Sands. *Dundee Courier*.

The accounts of the 1873 Open given in *The Field*, The *Fifeshire Journal* and The *St. Andrews Citizen* all say that conditions were perfect. The *Fifeshire Journal* has: 'For the game the weather could not have been more suited. It was dry. The sun was bright, and no wind disturbed the flight of the "gutta". The putting greens were in fair condition, and new holes had been cut . . .' The rest of that sentence is very important: '. . . but pools of water on the course added considerably to the hazards and militated against good scores'. *The Field* had: 'The course, however, was rather damp and in many places covered with water.' That would be bad enough; but in those days if you lifted your ball from casual water it cost you a stroke.

Hell Bunker. Here in 1978 Lanny Wadkins got down in 2 from the bunker for an 8. St. Andrews University, Cowie Collection.

The holder, young Tommy Morris, who had won for the fourth time at Prestwick in 1872, was the hot favourite, with Davie Strath, a great personal friend, as his closest rival. Only a few weeks before, they had been the centre of many golfers' attention as they played for £50 aside, six rounds in three days on St. Andrews Links. Young Tommy won by four and three, a contest which was evenly matched and full of fine golf. *The Field* ended its account: 'Towards the close of the contest the crowd had become so dense that the players could scarcely be picked up. All classes were represented, hundreds of strangers being present from all parts of the country, even England contributing its quota.' The other main contender was Jamie Anderson who was in fact runner-up this time to Tom Kidd; and he was to be a triple champion by 1879. He was a few years older than either young Tommy or Davie Strath – but alas, both were dead by that time.

As for Tom Kidd, he is first mentioned in 1871 as 'Young Tom Kidd,' to distinguish him from his father, Tom Kidd, senior, both their names appearing on a handwritten list of St.

Andrews' caddies sent to the R&A Secretary in 1875. The sender, R.T. Boothby ('The Major') enclosed a proof copy of 'The Rules . . . regarding Caddies,' which gave their rates as: First class 1/6d for the first round and 1/- for the second, or part of it; second class 1/- and then 6d. As a St. Andrews caddie Tom Kidd could not afford to travel much further than Elie, about twelve miles down the coast, when money prizes were available there. He did, however, defend his Championship at Musselburgh in 1874, and came a highly respectable eighth equal along with Bob Ferguson, later a triple Champion. In July 1872 he had partnered Davie Strath against Old and Young Tom Morris, and had beaten them: 'Kidd far exceeded his opponents in driving, his long swipes being much admired.'

There were twenty-six competitors in the 1873 Championship, several of them 'gentlemen amateurs,' and all but four of the professionals were local men. The pouring rain from Thursday to Saturday had probably deterred many distant players from coming forward. What always stands out in these Open Championships throughout the nineteenth century is the remarkable speed of play. This time they were supposed to start at 10am; but it was almost 10.30 before they were away – to play 36 holes with a break for lunch in early October! *The Field* reported:

> At the end of the first round the lowest scorers were: Bob Kirk, Jamie Anderson and Tom Kidd, each having accomplished the round at 91 strokes . . . At the end of the second round it was found that Tom Kidd was first with a total score of 179 strokes – 91 the first round and 88 the second – and he was accordingly declared 'champion' for the ensuing year, and received, in addition to the honour, the first money prize of £11 . . . Jamie Anderson was only one stroke behind him. In the second round coming home, Jamie was 'bunkered' in playing the 'heather hole,' and took nine to it. He also lost a shot in playing the last hole, through his second being in a bad position . . . As a whole the play may be justly characterised as far below the average. The driving was not so bad, but the putting was wretched.

The report added ironically: 'Whether the high scores were anticipated or not we cannot tell, but it is a significant fact that most of the markers were academic gentlemen, the arithmetic master being retained for Dr Argyll Robertson and Strath.'

The fairest summing-up came from the *Fifeshire Journal*: 'Kidd has been known for some years as an excellent player, and has recently been out in several important professional matches. At the same time, however, it was scarcely anticipated on Saturday morning that he would carry off the palm, although he might get a place in the prize list. As a player, he is likely to improve, especially in his short and quarter game.'

Kidd died on Wednesday, 16th January, 1884, and there was a brief account in the *Fifeshire Journal* the next day: 'Tom Kidd, who was well known on the Links, died very suddenly at his breakfast yesterday. Within the past few days he had been complaining of a pain in his chest. Dr Kyle stated that heart disease had been the cause of death. "Young Tom" who was thirty-five years of age, was the greater part of that time engaged as a caddie, and was a general favourite with the golfers.'

On Saturday, 19th January, 1884, the *St. Andrews Citizen* had: 'At Rose Lane, St Andrews, suddenly on the 16th inst. Thomas Kidd, junior, caddie and professional golfer, aged 36 years. Friends at a distance will please accept this intimation.'

On that Saturday, *The Field* published a fine obituary, which included the main information lacking in the two other notices: Kidd had been the 1873 Champion Golfer:

THE LATE TOM KIDD – Another well-known golfer has been removed, by the death of Tom Kidd, which took place suddenly at St. Andrews, on Wednesday. Kidd sprang, like so many exponents of golf, from an ancestry connected with the game, and was thus brought up, so to speak, with a club in his hand. He was one of the many professional players who, some ten years ago, brought professional play in St. Andrews into such high repute. Among these were the well-known names of Tom Morris, elder and younger, Davie Strath, and Jamie Anderson, then so often pitted against each other in single and foursome play. In 1873 one of the latter contests took place in a match, which excited considerable interest – Tom Morris, jun., and Jamie Anderson against Strath and Kidd, over three rounds of St. Andrews; and, although the former were victors by four holes out of the fifty-four, it is doubtful whether such an exhibition of foursome playing was ever

The shared 5th and 13th greens. Said to be the largest double green in the world. St. Andrews University, Cowie Collection.

witnessed, the average of the three rounds being a little over 85. In the same year Kidd won the championship at St. Andrews, which had been reinstituted the year previous, when it was won for the fourth time in succession by Tom Morris, jun. In competitions, both on his own and other greens, Kidd was generally among the prize winners, and as late as 1882 he took the first prize at Elie. Although somewhat ungainly in his style of play, he was a powerful driver, and understood the game well and how it should be played. He thus became the instructor of many a novice who came to St. Andrews to acquire the art, and he will be long remembered for the pains he took in instilling into his pupils the importance of the 'grip' of the club and the 'stand' to the ball, no less than for his civil and obliging disposition.

CHAPTER 5

1876 – THE WALK-OVER CHAMPIONSHIP

WHEN PRINCE LEOPOLD DROVE HIMSELF IN AS CAPTAIN in late September 1876 he was the first 'Royal' to do so. His older brother the Prince of Wales, later Edward VII, had been similarly honoured in 1863, but had delegated his duties to John Whyte Melville, a distinguished R&A Past Captain, and did not come to St. Andrews at all. Leopold was actually a golfer. His physician after playing at Carnoustie in Summer 1871 had recommended golf as a healthful pursuit for the Prince, and a delighted Carnoustie clubmaker had had to despatch four sets of clubs to Windsor Castle. The programme of the 1876 Autumn Meeting was perfectly normal; but the Prince's visit resulted in a cut-back in actual golfing time for the R&A Members. This probably affected the turnout of golfers on the Saturday, the last day of the Autumn Meeting when the competition to find the champion golfer was decided.

Prince Leopold, 1876, flanked by Old Tom Morris and John Whyte Melville, who actually drove in for the Prince of Wales in 1863.

TWO PHASES OF GOLF.

"'FORE!'"   "'HIND!'"

Hazards of golf, Victorian-style.

Nowadays the driving-in ceremony takes place at the traditional hangman's hour of 8am; even in these earlier days it usually happened at 10am to allow the last of the competitors for the Medals to complete their rounds in more or less daylight. But on that Wednesday in 1876 Prince Leopold arrived at 11 and drove himself into office about 11.15 watched by 'thousands of spectators comprising the elite of the County'. It must have been about 11.45 before the huge crowd had dispersed sufficiently to allow the Autumn Meeting to get under way. Nowadays a slow game can take 5¼ hours to complete 18 holes; that was how long it took all forty-eight couples to play out the 1876 competition. On the Thursday the Prince arrived about noon, played a short six-hole match with old Tom as his partner, and after lunch proceeded to the ladies' course, the Himalayas putting green, where about fifty R&A Members were joining in a competition with their wives. Normally that would have taken place during the previous week, but now more golfing time was lost. On Friday, *The Field* reported: 'Several interesting matches were played, but the Prince having departed by the forenoon train, the remainder of the morning to a great degree was shorn of its interest.'

Until now there had been no problem with the Professional Tournament on the Saturday, not only in 1873 when Kidd won the Championship. In 1871, when there was no championship at Prestwick, £26 had been contributed by R&A Members for a St. Andrews Tournament; and each year from then they provided an average of almost £30 for the same purpose. But on Saturday, 30th September, 1876 the situation was almost farcical. Large numbers of R&A Members were playing off, and the championship competitors had to go off alternately with them! *The St. Andrews Citizen* said: 'The members of the Royal & Ancient might have exercised that courtesy which is invariably accorded them on their Medal days.' That ignored the fact that the R&A were actually running this Championship, and perhaps in all the excitement of Prince Leopold's visit had forgotten to arrange to have the use of the Course that day. The curtailment of golf during the Prince's stay in St. Andrews may also have been a factor. Whatever the reasons, it meant that the Course was so crowded by golfers and spectators as to disrupt the play. Often several of the couples had to stand waiting before they could play up to the putting greens; and this led to a miserable dispute over the final result.

Young Tommy Morris had lost his young wife and their baby in childbirth just a year before; and on Christmas Day 1875 he had been found dead having burst a blood vessel. In these sad circumstances his great friend David Strath now started favourite in 1876. But many fancied Bob Martin, another local man who had already been close to winning the Championship. He was partnered by Tom Kidd, a possible winner. What a contrast in styles they presented: Strath with his smooth effortless swing; Kidd with his lengthy but ungainly 'swipes'; and Martin who himself described his flat swing as 'like an auld wife cutting hay'.

Much space in contemporary accounts was given to the pairing of Old Tom Morris and Willie Park, Senior. After all, their series of great matches went back more than twenty years. But although at fifty-five Tom was still a fine performer, and Park was in fact the holder, the real struggle was between Davie Strath and Bob Martin. Both he and Martin took 86 for the first round, there the one notable incident being the careless missing of a two-inch putt on the 15th green by Strath. In the last five holes his second round became a nightmare. R&A Members were not the only ones to be holding up the Course. We are told in various books that Strath hit a spectator and laid him out. What really happened was this. Davie's second shot at the long 14th struck Mr Hutton, Upholsterer, who was playing out, on the forehead, and he fell to the ground. Mr Hutton, though stunned, was later able to walk home. *The St. Andrews*

Bob Martin, Open Champion 1876 and 1885.

Citizen then provided this understatement: 'This seemed to shake Davie a little bit, for this hole and also the next he did in six strokes.'

When Strath began the last two holes, the crowd had increased to hundreds and it was known that Bob Martin with a second round of 90 had left Strath this target: 10 to win, 11 to tie. He played two excellent shots down the 17th and was left with a long iron to the green. By now the crowd was very thick although the *Citizen*'s reporter could still follow the play; while those in front were still putting, Strath, assisted by the wind, played a fine shot to the green, striking someone near the hole, 'which of course checked its forward career'. (Otherwise it would have been on the road.) Davie holed in five. No-one seemed to have told him at that point that someone had lodged an objection and wished to have him disqualified for playing his ball up to the hole side while putting was going on. 'The crowd so increased during the playing of the last hole that it was impossible for us to get near the players, and it must have been trying for Strath. He holed in six strokes' – and tied with Martin.

The objection was to be referred to the Council of the Royal and Ancient. Another charge had been levelled at Strath: that his card had not been accurately kept by the marker – one of those specially provided by the R&A – but they would surely have supported him had it been necessary. Strath and Martin were told to play off the tie on the Monday before any decision had been reached. Strath refused to take part in the play-off in these circumstances; Martin walked over the Course and was declared the winner. He was then and is now the only winner of a St. Andrews Open to finish 7, 5.

Screeds and screeds were written at the time sympathising with Strath, a special point being made that 'If Strath did infringe a Rule of the Club, that Rule was infringed repeatedly on Saturday . . .' In Cousins and Scott's *A Century of Opens* they say:

We cannot trace the existence of a Rule penalising a golfer for driving into players in front, although the Rules at that date had local variations and there might conceivably have been one at St. Andrews on those lines. This we doubt, and believe that Strath's offence was against the etiquette of the game.

In the main body of the St. Andrews Rules under the heading of II – Place of Teeing exactly the same words are used in 1851, 1858 and 1875 – the Rules in force: 'When two parties meet on the Putting Green, the party first there may claim the privilege of holing out, and any party coming up must wait until the other party has played out the hole, and on no account play their balls up lest they should annoy the parties who are putting.' Poor Strath must have known that once that rule was invoked he would be disqualified. The fact that it had not been invoked on several occasions earlier in the day is irrelevant.

Davie Strath had no real chance again of becoming champion golfer, as his brother Andrew had done in 1865. When he left for Australia in 1879 he was dying of consumption just as Andrew had been when he too had gone there in the hope of restoring his health.

CHAPTER 6

A VERY COLOURFUL TRIPLE CHAMPION: JAMIE ANDERSON

HEN THE CHAMPIONSHIP RETURNED TO ST. ANDREWS LINKS in late September, 1879, Jamie Anderson was a strong favourite to win for the third year in a row. In 1877 at Musselburgh he had played very steadily and won by two shots; but he needed a tremendous finish in the 1878 Prestwick Open. 'Jof' (James Ogilvy Fairlie) Morris had finished at 161, leaving Jamie with the daunting task of completing the last four holes in 17 strokes. That would be considered a good normal score – merely to tie. 5, 4, 3, 5 was needed. Jamie holed a full iron shot for a three at the fifteenth, sank a putt right across the green for a four at the sixteenth, had a one at the short seventeenth, and a safe five at the last. That made a total of thirteen – and he won – but only by two shots, from Bob Kirk, who had had a splendid final round. So in fact he had needed fifteen to tie, which might have daunted even him. His one at the seventeenth was a remarkable affair. He had tee'd his ball just in front of the box. A spectator who was supposed to be backing another competitor said just as Jamie began to address his ball, 'If that man plays that ball he will be disqualified'. Jamie stopped, had a walk around to collect himself, re-tee'd the ball to everyone's satisfaction, and put it straight in the hole! 'Thank ye, sir,' said Jamie, 'I'm muckle obliged to ye.' It was in these brave but rather lucky circumstances that he was able to try for a third successive Open.

You could always tell it was Young Tommy Morris if you saw him at a distance playing a long shot: he waggled the club a great many times and then with the force of the strike his Balmoral bonnet would probably leave his head. Jamie Anderson was not a long driver and his brilliant short game was his forte; but he too was instantly recognisable – from the speed of his play. He seemed to have decided long before he reached his ball exactly what he aimed to do, and on reaching it he at once sent it on its way. He took his stance in a second, had one look at the hole and with no waggles at all hit it truly and well.

There was a record entry of 46 for the 1879 Open, and apart from Jamie Anderson there were several strong contenders including Jamie Allan, the Prestwick man who had become the professional at Westward Ho! in a remote corner of Devon. Anderson and Allan were to have a great match on two Scottish and two English courses for several hundreds of pounds once the Championship was over; but there was a close-fought battle before that. No one fancied the chances of a nineteen-year-old called Andra Kirkaldy but he was second eventually and was to figure again and again in golf history, although he never won the Championship.

Jamie. Allan, an early starter, soon had to demonstrate that, although the Swilcan Burn in

Jamie Anderson, a very colourful Triple Champion.

front of the first green was a difficult water hazard, it was then possible to play out of it. 'Rolling up his trousers, he pluckily stepped into the stream', played a good iron shot onto the green and got his five. In 1879 most of the journalists seem to have followed Allan in the first round and Anderson for most of the second, giving a hole-by-hole account, nowadays the province of the Club bore. But several interesting points emerge. The word 'drove' is used again and again to describe an iron shot from rough or a bad lie. This 'heavy' iron called a 'niblick' was used for driving the ball forward. It was a 'steal' if you holed an unlikely putt from a distance; a 'gobble', however, was a rapid straight putt into the hole so that, had it not gone in it would have been well past. In those days apart from the driver, or play club, there were other wooden clubs called 'spoons', because their faces were concave, and with them you could achieve various lofted shots, especially by slicing across the ball from right to left. The equivalent of a two-wood came in about this time, because a glossary in the 1882 Rules gives a 'brassy', so called because the complete sole was covered by a brass plate to protect it when playing fairway shots. Clearly there was much room for manufacturing shots then, whereas a modern matched set puts a premium on accurate striking.

After the first round Jamie Anderson was in the lead with an 84, Andra Kirkaldy was next at 86, Tom Kidd third at 87, and Jamie Allan and Kinsman were at 88. Jamie Anderson's magnificent temperament is brought out in what follows; Jamie Allan's is not, although the newspaper account may be at fault in that respect. After all, Allan was a Prestwick man playing out of an English Club – and that may have caused some bias. We are told that the large following which Allan had had in the morning melted away in the afternoon because there were several lower scores. That seemed more of an advantage than a drawback, especially when he went out in 38, the lowest score for the first nine all day. Very soon he drew a large following once more, 'which seemed to tell upon his play, and he did not show so well in the home coming'. He took 46 which included a seven and a six. Jamie Anderson after his 84 found a large gallery for his second round; 'Jamie, however, is accustomed to being lionised, and the presence of the multitude did not in any way disturb his equanimity, and he continued his quiet and steady game.' He was out in 41 as in his first round. He too had a seven and a six near the start of the inward half, and then knew that he had to do the last five holes in good figures to win. He did exactly that, could have taken six at the last but had a very good four and won by three shots. Kirkaldy had tied with Jamie Allan for second and just managed to win the play-off by a single shot.

In this year, 1879, there is a fascinating link between Jamie Anderson and two of the greatest Open Champions, John Henry Taylor and James Braid, who will figure largely, later in the story. Taylor was born and bred in Northam, near Westward Ho! in Devon, Braid in Earlsferry, Fife, a dozen miles from St. Andrews. They were both nine at this time. Each was then greatly influenced by Jamie Anderson. Taylor recalled when he had seen him play in a foursome at Westward Ho! shortly after his great match with Jamie Allan had ended in victory for the champion. Anderson and 'Jof' Morris (who was his caddie) played Jamie Allan and his brother Johnnie:

> The game was a very close one, and playing to, I think, the fourteenth hole, Morris's ball off the tee shot lay on the extreme edge of a bunker, leaving Anderson with only enough standing room for his right foot (without a stance for his left, it was impossible to play at the hole). Not to be beaten, however, Anderson called for volunteers, and a man named Burch (the late Sexton of Northam) stepped forward, and stooping down so that his back was on a level with the edge of the bunker, Anderson planted his left foot firmly on it, and playing a grand shot put the ball on the green, thereby winning the hole and the match . . .'
> Taylor added: 'It was, without doubt, my very first introduction to first-class golf . . . I sometimes wonder what would be said if such a thing was done in a first-class match at the present time . . .   *(December 31, 1897)*

Jamie Anderson died in August, 1905, not in '1912' as stated in two encyclopedias. James Braid had just become Open Champion at St. Andrews in 1905 and, shortly before Jamie's death, he recalled in *Golf Illustrated* a match at Elie, Fife, in 1879. As a nine-year-old, Braid had watched the great Anderson, then Open Champion. He had followed Jamie all over the links and when he was not otherwise engaged the little boy showed him some of the shots of which he was capable. 'I followed him around like a little dog,' said Braid, 'gazing with admiration at everything he did . . .' Jamie in his turn took some notice of and interest in Braid and after watching him make a few shots he told him very seriously that if he went in thoroughly for golf he would himself one day be the Open Champion. Braid never forgot what he said and it remained the most vivid remembrance of his boyhood. Jamie's obituary in *Golf Illustrated* ended with these words: 'Thus the Open Champion who has gone may have been, in a sense, the making of the Open Champion who bears the distinction today.'

CHAPTER 7

1882 – A GREAT MUSSELBURGH CHAMPION: BOB FERGUSON

WHEN MUSSELBURGH IS MENTIONED, the first name to spring to mind is 'Park': Willie Park Senior, four times Champion Golfer between 1860 and 1875; and Willie Park Junior, Champion in 1887 and 1889. But just as Jamie Anderson is a proud St. Andrews name for three good Open reasons, so Bob Ferguson's is revered at Musselburgh. His first victory, at Musselburgh in 1880, was slightly clouded by the absence of Anderson, the holder, said to be due to short notice being given of the Championship. But on his home course, Ferguson was always likely to win. He had in fact been third at Prestwick as long ago as 1869 when he was 21, but through an unfortunate misprint that fine performance has sometimes been credited to an amateur, 'Mr S. Mure Fergusson, Royal & Ancient'. At Prestwick in 1881 he had won by three shots from Jamie Anderson; at St. Andrews in 1882 he was the man to beat. It was typical of Ferguson that his form in practice the day before the Championship had been 'vile beyond description'; but as he was quoted as saying, 'It didna matter as I dinna lose anything'. In a money match he was determination personified.

Weather conditions for the 1882 Championship were very fine; there were no pools of water as in 1873 to militate against good scoring. But now the Royal and Ancient had published a revised set of Rules, and they made conditions decidedly more difficult. For the diameter of the hole was defined as four inches; from then until the 1891 revision – and so in 1885 and 1888 – it remained like that. In 1891 and ever since, the diameter has been four and a quarter inches. When you consider also the state of the greens after several days' heavy traffic during the Autumn Meeting, before the Championship on the Saturday, and know that the gutta ball was on average slightly bigger than the modern one, there were three factors making putting more difficult. The winning score in 1882, 1885 and 1888 was 171. Not too much can be read into it, but in 1891 the winner took 166; in 1895 the average for two of the four rounds was 161; and in 1900, 154.5. That was still with the gutta; soon the core-wound rubber ball, the Haskell, would add twenty or thirty yards to shots through the green.

The outstanding feature of the 1882 Championship was the fine performances from three amateur players: Mr. Fitz Boothby, St. Andrews, who was equal third alongside two Champions, Anderson and Martin; Mr. James Mansfield of Edinburgh who tied with Willie Park Senior for seventh place; and Mr. Henry Lamb of Edinburgh, who came next, tied with Tom Kidd. In recent years only one amateur had really distinguished himself: appropriately enough it was Mr. John Ball, Junior, who in 1878 had at the age of fifteen tied for fourth place with Bob Martin, and not unnaturally lost the play-off over the round of twelve holes. The fifth prize was thirty shillings, and Ball, the first amateur to become Champion Golfer, in 1890, was thoroughly

Bob Ferguson, a triple and almost quadruple Champion.

ill-advised by a well-meaning adult – and accepted it. However, he was adjudged to have been innocently misled.

In 1882, although it was early October and there were forty competitors, the usual starting-time of 10 a.m. was observed. Tom Morris, who did not play, acted as starter and gave 'a word of encouragement to each, in his usual happy kind of way as they struck off from the tee'. Ferguson and Anderson, present and past champions, were obviously favourites; but lurking there were Bob Martin, Tom Kidd and Mr. Fitz Boothby – all known to be in good form. Willie Fernie, a St. Andrean, and later a famous professional at Troon, was also fancied. His turn was to come the following year when he tied with Bob Ferguson at Musselburgh, and in the play-off was a shot behind coming to the last short hole. There he holed a long 'steal' for a two,

Ferguson took four, and was thus robbed of a fourth consecutive win which would have equalled young Tommy's record. But Fernie was second this time.

In the first round the main gallery went with Jamie Anderson and Bob Martin, and the usual shot-by-shot account was forthcoming. Jamie played beautifully as far as the thirteenth but then he had consecutive sevens and finished with an 87, four shots behind Ferguson. Mr. Fitz Boothby had an 86, as did Jack Kirkaldy of that St. Andrews family. Tom Kidd had taken 87 and complained bitterly of his luck, which drew from *The Field* a rather acid comment: 'He attempted too much, and more cautious play might have advanced his interests more.' Mr. Mansfield, playing with Kidd, had a 91, and Mr. Henry Lamb an 88.

After his 83, Ferguson took the main gallery in the afternoon. A highlight of his round was a three at the 11th where he was in the dreaded Strath bunker at the front of the green. He came out well and holed a fine putt to 'hearty applause'. When he came to the 15th it was described as the 'ginger-beer hole'; that is where you might want a drink – certainly more than at what is now called 'Ginger Beer' – the 4th. Bob Ferguson's 88 gave him 171, good enough to beat Fernie by three shots, Jamie Anderson, Bob Martin, Jack Kirkaldy and Mr. Fitz Boothby by four. There were several ties for the nine prizes ranging in value from £12 to 15/-, but they were not played off, 'the money being in each case divided. Mr. Boothby, Mr. Mansfield and Mr. Henry Lamb only playing for "honour", Rennie and Kidd got a place on the prize list'.

After losing so narrowly to Fernie at Musselburgh in 1883, Bob Ferguson's name does not appear in the results given for Prestwick in 1884 and St. Andrews in 1885. He may perhaps, like Tom Kidd, have found it too expensive to travel from Musselburgh. He was fourth equal at Musselburgh in 1886, but by 1889 and the next Championship there he had had a serious illness, and was never quite the same man. For a time he was greenkeeper at Musselburgh; but from the 1890s on he was prominent as a caddie to various fine amateurs, and professionals too. In a splendid panoramic photograph of the first green at St. Andrews during an epic match between Andra Kirkaldy and Willie Park Junior in 1890, Bob the triple Champion Golfer is seen with Park's clubs under his arm.

CHAPTER 8

AN ALLEGED ELEVEN
AT THE ROAD HOLE: 1885

*B*EFORE DISCUSSING A VERY MYSTERIOUS ELEVEN AT THE SEVENTEENTH in the 1885 Open, it will be as well to take in some earlier inaccuracies, and to clarify one or two other points.

The report on each of the Championships is preceded by a summary of the results so far; in 1885 there were misleading statements. We are told that after 'Young Tommy' won 'about 1869' for the third time the belt became his absolute property. Then we get: 'The meeting lapsed for some three years but was again inaugurated on a more permanent basis . . .' We know perfectly well that it lapsed for one year, 1871. Further down we are told that in 1883 William Fernie won at Musselburgh and 'proved more than a match for all his opponents'. This is a strange way of describing a tie between Bob Ferguson of Musselburgh and Fernie, the St. Andrean, a tie broken only at the thirty-sixth hole of the play-off when a monstrous 'steal' by Fernie robbed Ferguson of a further battle. For 1884, we are told that Jack Simpson 'occupied the premier position' at Prestwick. Local knowledge could be largely discounted because from 1883 onwards the course had been extensively altered and there were now eighteen holes there. Jack Simpson, like the illustrious James Braid, was born and bred in Earlsferry, the other half of Elie in Fife. Coming 22 miles along the coast from St. Andrews, you first enter the small town of Elie; if you play the first two holes on Elie Links you are faced with a shot of about 200 yards downhill to a green with a wall behind it. Carry that wall, and you are in Earlsferry! It was on the next fairway, the fourth, that Jack Simpson and James Braid would hit their very first golf ball, long before I did, in 1925. Now it is time to return to Bob Martin and St. Andrews.

In 1876 when Bob Martin had won at St. Andrews it was in very controversial circumstances: Davie Strath had tied with him, but had conceded a walk-over. This bears no relation to the report given in Mortimer and Pignon's *Story of the Open Championship: 1860-1950* where we get half a sentence on Bob Martin's 1876 win followed by details relating to the 1878 Open at Prestwick!

In 1876, when Bob Martin of St. Andrews won on his own links with a total of 176, J.O.F. Morris, the youngest son of Old Tom, came within an ace of victory and then, alas! threw away his chance. He had only to do a couple of sixes to win; however, we all know the terrors of the 17th hole at St. Andrews and, on this occasion poor Morris took a nine and followed it with a six at the 18th – and all was over!

However, we know that the Road Hole played no part that year, except in allowing Martin with a seven there to become Champion.

Early 1890s 'transitional': one caddy still carries the clubs loose under-arm, the other carries a bag.

It did seem in 1885 that a terrible disaster at the 17th had struck Davie Ayton, the St. Andrews professional – for Bob Martin, the winner, tells us so:

I won the Open Championship honour twice. The first time was in 1876, and the second in 1885, both at St. Andrews with scores of 176 and 171 respectively. But on the latter occasion I must say I had a bit of good luck, or rather perhaps I should put it this way, that Davie Ayton had it extraordinarily bad. He finished second to me, only two shots behind, and that was after he had actually taken eleven strokes to the 17th hole. I can quite well remember how it was that he did so. He had played his first and second shots both capitally; his third, the approach to the hole, was also a good one, but was just a trifle short and landing on the face of the green it ran along it and lay close in behind that small bunker which guards the hole there; his fourth, a pitch over that hazard, was too

40

strong and went on to the road at the other side of the green, he took two more to get it off there, but only to go into that self-same bunker, and it then cost him the remaining five strokes to extricate himself from it and hole out. So that, but for his third shot there being a little weak, he would easily have been Open Champion that year instead of me.

Between January 1891 and February 1893 most of the early Champion Golfers had been invited to write about their careers in *Golf*. Significantly enough, there had been twenty-five autobiographies from the gentlemen amateurs and only fourteen from the professionals. But Bob Martin's account was in *Golf Illustrated* on 20th April, 1906, thirty years after his first Open win, and over twenty since his second. And none of the contemporary 1885 reports on the Championship bear out a word of what he said about Davie Ayton's performance. The simple facts were these. Ayton took 89 in the first round, out in 45 and back in 44 – no room for an eleven there. He in fact finished 6, 4, and since Archie Simpson had managed an 83, and Martin an 84, Ayton was never in a position to be five shots ahead during the second round,

Golfers patronising Old Daw's ginger pop and milk stall, c. 1880. He also made lemon drinks from the fruit seen on top of the barrow. *Evening Telegraph*, Dundee.

The first green during an epic match between Andra Kirkaldy and Willie Park Junior in 1890. Bob Ferguson the Triple Champion is seen with Park's clubs under his arm.

The Dawn of Golf.

only to throw it all away. (That has been the story ever since.) He in fact had a very good 84; it would have required a miracle to do that with an eleven on the card.

Bob Martin had worked for Jamie Anderson as a clubmaker presumably in the 1870s since he mentions Jamie's having come over to him from his shop when Bob, still in his teens, was sitting at the back of the home green at the end of a caddying day. Jamie had engaged him on the spot; then, after his apprenticeship Bob had left to work for Forgan; soon after that, for the next twenty years he was with Tom Morris. However, that had ended in November, 1902 when he had been badly injured in a fall from a cart. His golfing days were long over, and from then on he went back to caddying, much less arduous than standing at a clubmaker's bench. It was in these circumstances that, in 1906, he had been invited to reminisce. Presumably it had been far too long ago, with far too many professional tournaments at St. Andrews following the autumn meeting for him to remember the details. The R&A Members had been extremely generous in contributing an average of £25 each year.

Bob Martin would probably be far more interested in the money than in the base-metal Open medal, and 1876 and 1885 would not stand out particularly in his memory. He had been wrong also when he said that Davie Ayton was second in 1885. That honour had belonged to Archie Simpson who, at 172, had come between Martin and Ayton. Ayton had another claim to fame: 'He began his career as a participator in great matches by carrying the clubs of Young Tom Morris in all his principal engagements.'

A main feature in the 1882 Championship had been the fine performance by three gentlemen amateurs. This time no professional had to suffer the humiliation of gaining a prize because an amateur was playing only for the 'honour'. But two of the very famous amateurs, Horace Hutchinson and John Ball Junior, only just failed to produce such a situation.

However, we must again wait for the first time when the Road Hole played a decisive part in deciding the winner of an Open Championship.

CHAPTER 9

A SCORECARD
ADDED UP WRONGLY: 1888

BEFORE GIVING AN ACCOUNT OF THE 1888 CHAMPIONSHIP it is as well for the sake of continuity to discuss very briefly the 1886 Open at Musselburgh, and the 1887 one at Prestwick. In 1886 David Brown, a plasterer from Musselburgh, won on his home links with a score of 157, the lowest to date on that course. It was fitting, however, that a far more famous Champion, Willie Park Junior, reduced that record to 155 in 1889 – as did Andra Kirkaldy – and Park won the resultant play-off. Their joint record stands forever because in 1892 the Honourable Company moved to Muirfield, and Musselburgh was no longer a Championship venue. When Park won at Prestwick in 1887, by far the best performance by any amateur until then came from Mr John E. Laidlay who was fourth. In the next ten years two famous amateurs were to win the Open once and twice respectively: John Ball Junior and Harold H. Hilton.

There was amazingly little publicity in advance of the 1888 Championship even though a change without precedent had been made. This time it was played on the Saturday following the Autumn Meeting; but a notice in *The Scotsman* on Saturday, 22nd September was 'the first and only insertion regarding the Championship'. A letter at this time signed by Tom Morris – and no doubt written by his helpful son 'Jof' – maintained that the host Club had every right to switch the Championship to a week after the Autumn Meeting 'so that everyone can enjoy a clear green and to suit as many golfers as possible'. As we shall see, in 1891 strenuous efforts were made to suit just one person, the Champion Golfer of 1890.

In 1888 at St. Andrews the weather made scoring very difficult. A cold north wind was blowing, and going out the players had to drive right in the teeth of it. The greens were very keen and as the *Fifeshire Journal* put it: 'On this account the putting was by no means so brilliant. On several occasions the ball would run round the hole or stop just as it was about to go in.' Clearly some of these putts would have been dropping had the hole been quarter of an inch bigger in diameter as it would be at the 1891 Open, and from then on.

Before play began there were several strong favourites including Willie Campbell, a well-known Musselburgh player, and Hugh Kirkaldy, Andra's younger brother, who had recently holed the links in 74 strokes. Willie Park Junior was not greatly fancied even although he was the holder. Young Archie Simpson had defeated him heavily not so long ago, and seemed a better bet. Archie and Robert as well as Jack Simpson the 1884 Champion were among six brothers born in Earlsferry; their names were later associated more with Carnoustie where Robert Simpson became a well-known clubmaker. Young Archie Simpson put himself well out of the running with an opening 91; and Hugh Kirkaldy for all his recent 74 was to take 98. Another favourite, the 1883 Champion, Willie Fernie, took over 90 for each round on this, his

John Burns, Warwick, Champion 1888, his medal gilt base metal.

Ben Sayers at the finish of a running approach shot.

native links. You may also judge of the conditions when Jamie Anderson, that great triple champion, but now 46 and a very busy clubmaker, took 96 followed by a 99 and was 24 shots behind the winner.

The winner was not easy to spot. Ben Sayers, who had received no pre-Championship mention, came in with a total of 172 and it was thought that he had won. But soon afterwards in came Davie Anderson, St. Andrews and Jack Burns, also a St. Andrean, each with a total equalling Sayers', 172. It seemed that a play-off was assured. But, as only the *Fifeshire Journal* explained clearly, 'It so happened that as a member of the Royal and Ancient Golf Club was looking over the cards in the Clubhouse he found that the figures on Jack Burns' card had through some mistake or other been added up wrongly . . .' The *Journal* says that his second round total had been made 86 instead of the actual 85; other sources say his first round had been totalled at 87 instead of 86. Whatever the truth is, and however unfortunate for Sayers and Anderson, the mistake could not be disputed, and it was ultimately decided that Jack Burns was the Champion Golfer, 1888.

The new Champion required considerable strength to battle against the conditions that day. He is described as 'a young player full of vigour and sturdiness' and 'a strapping young fellow'. But he needed much more than that to equal Bob Martin's winning score in 1885, made in 'pretty favourable conditions'. We are told that 'He had played an all-round game driving long and sure, handling the iron well (note the singular!), and putting deadly'. Burns, like Brown the 1886 Champion, was a plasterer to trade; but at the time of his win he was Greenkeeper and Professional to the Warwick Golf Club, instituted as recently as November, 1886. That appointment would have been arranged by a very well known Royal and Ancient Member, Colonel R.T. Boothby, because he was President of the Warwick Club. Burns did not remain there long. The 1887-8 *Golfing Annual* mentions no greenkeeper at that time; in 1888-9 it says, 'Greenkeeper – John Burns, champion golfer for 1888-1889'; in 1889-90 there is 'Greenkeeper – John Burns, ex champion golfer'. The following year Gerald Farrar became greenkeeper. Because of one of many gems in Webster Evans' *Encyclopaedia of Golf* we know what happened to Burns after that. He must have had a very nice sense of humour:

> After winning, he gave up his occupation as a plasterer and became professional at the Warwick Club. After some years, he returned to St. Andrews and worked as a platelayer on the railway. When asked how he was playing, he used to reply: 'Never better – I haven't been off the line for years!'

CHAPTER 10

HUGH KIRKALDY'S WIN: 1891

*I*N 1889 THE VERY COLOURFUL ANDRA KIRKALDY* had again come within an ace of winning the Championship. For steadiness and brilliance combined his game could hardly have been excelled; and when he returned a record 155 at Musselburgh the score seemed unassailable. But Willie Park Junior, playing brilliantly too, eventually needed a three to tie. A throng of spectators were far too close to the hole, but although his ball actually touched one of them, it is doubtful whether that helped him at all. His first putt was stone-dead, and a complete replay over 36 holes followed. Andra was for once off his driving, and lost by five

John Ball Jr., first amateur Open Champion 1890, by Hodge.

shots. However, very few men had taken on the great Musselburgh players on their home green and achieved a tie – especially in a record score.

The next year, 1890, was epoch-making. For the first time an amateur, John Ball Junior – an Englishman at that – wrested the title from the Scots who had monopolised it for thirty years. There had been little indication of a breakthrough; a fourth place for Laidlay had been the best before that – and most times the amateurs had failed to make any professional gain a money prize by default. But Ball had been raised at Hoylake, and having played it in a gale of wind during the Centenary celebrations of the Amateur Championship in 1985, I can vouch for it as an excellent preparation for doing battle in bad weather on any Scottish links. Prestwick, where Ball won, was noted for the number of its blind shots; but even in a strong North-West wind there in 1890, the great amateur was capable of golf which left little to chance. His eight Amateur Championships will surely be an all-time record.

Now, in 1891 at St. Andrews, it would be the last time the Championship was decided over 36 holes. Here too for the first time the diameter of the hole had officially grown to four and a quarter inches, surely a considerable factor in allowing championship scores to become on average lower.

Only a month before the 1891 Open, Thomas Owen Potter, the distinguished Secretary of the Royal Liverpool Club, Hoylake, had written to the Royal and Ancient complaining that the Champion golfer, John Ball Junior, would be unable to defend his title on 6th October because of a clash with Hoylake's autumn meeting! The R&A did try to shift the date to 26th September, and that would have resolved a clash not only with Hoylake but with Prestwick and Westward Ho!; but it was too late.

There was a record entry of over eighty, almost double the number competing at either Musselburgh or Prestwick in the most recent Championships. For that number of players, even starting at 9 a.m., 36 holes of card and pencil golf on an October day was decidedly a tall order. Instructions to competitors were very brief:

> Play will commence in the First Round at 9 a.m. and in the Second Round at 12.15 p.m.
> Parties not present when their names are called will be placed at the bottom of the list.
> Approved Markers must be provided.
> As the days are short it is particularly requested that all Competitors will play with as little delay as possible.
>
> *By Order of the Green Committee.*

In the event, the afternoon round got underway at 12.30 p.m. – not bad, three and a half hours to play their round and have their lunch! But in spite of the rule about 'Approved Markers' there were many complaints that experienced golfers had preferred to watch the play, leaving schoolboys to act as markers. The days were indeed short so that Willie Fernie the 1883 Champion was decidedly unfortunate in the ballot for partners since he went out second last. It was worse for Davie Brown, the 1886 Champion, and Willie Auchterlonie, soon to win his Open, the final pairing. For English competitors the main drawback was that only *The Field* carried the necessary details about the Championship, a more expensive magazine than professionals could then usually afford. As a result about ten players were allowed in only under protest from other competitors – a poor atmosphere in which to produce good golf. The

Freddie Tait at the finish of his swing.

need to reduce the field was obvious; and the *Golfing Annual* had already in 1890 made a sensible suggestion:

> . . . a prohibitive entry fee might deter many amateur players with little or no chance of success from entering, and at the same time a large sum of money could thereby be provided for division among the leading professionals.

Other radical reforms were needed, especially a move from autumn to summer; by 1895 when the Championship returned to St. Andrews, it took place in June.

The 1891 field was very strong: Willie Fernie now of Troon had been in splendid form; Bob Martin, Davie Brown the 1886 Champion, Willie Park Junior and Archie Simpson were all

Hugh Kirkaldy, Champion 1891.

Hugh Kirkaldy, by Hodge.

likely to come in high. And after his performance in 1890, Ball was rated very highly, especially in the prevailing weather conditions on that Tuesday – wretched, with drenching rain and against a strong easterly wind. Old Tom's choice was Hugh Kirkaldy because he felt that, if he kept to his usual powerful game, he would beat the field. In recent years he had lowered the record from 77, made by Young Tommy nineteen years before, to 74. The most astonishing feature of that round was the outward half of 33: seven 4's with a three at the seventh and a two at the eighth. This was with a gutta ball which flew twenty to thirty yards shorter than the Haskell which would displace it in a few years' time. Some favoured Hugh's older brother, Andra, a very powerful driver, and probably the most determined of all the St. Andrews players.

Ball was out early and seemed to be heading for at least a reasonable first round when disaster struck at the Road Hole. A long brassy shot carried over the road into a ditch where it lay so badly that after a couple of ineffectual attempts to get out he was compelled to lift and lose a couple of strokes. The result was a horrendous eleven. Fernie knocked three strokes off Jack Burns' record 1888 total of 171, in even poorer conditions. His two 84s were matched by Andra Kirkaldy, very fine indeed. But his brother Hugh was in even better form. His driving was splendid: at the eighteenth with his gutta ball he was over the road against the wind. His total of 166 broke the record by five shots. Andra had needed two very difficult fours to win but had finished 5, 6. He had some consolation when he defeated Fernie in the play-off for second and third place, and so we had two brothers occupying the two leading places for the first, but not, as we shall see, the only time.

There is a legend that Andra deliberately allowed Hugh to win, because his brother was in poor health and would soon suffer the same fate as the Straths. Although Andra agreed that he had played the last two holes badly, he insisted that he had tried his hardest to win. In any case, long after this 1891 Open in January 1894 Hugh demonstrated that he positively thrived in adverse conditions. Did he not thrash Frederick Guthrie Tait, the great amateur, and a very tough physical training instructor, in early January when a piercingly cold wind penetrated the marrow and blew constantly with the force of half a gale? He seemed to enjoy the Arctic conditions, his only concession to the weather being a scarf round his neck; but Tait was paralysed by the cold and lost over 36 holes by 11 and 9. There was no sign of ill-health there; but Hugh was fated to die young. A particularly virulent strain of influenza laid him low in April 1896, and as it became clear that he had suffered irreparable damage to his lungs, the golfing world rallied round with money to support him, his young wife and child. He was a particularly likeable young man: 'Hugh showed himself possessed of many excellent qualities, unfailing good humour in diverse critical situations . . . than whom a more popular golfer whether professional or amateur probably never struck a ball'. It is Hugh Kirkaldy's dashing style that is figured on the cover of the Badminton book on Golf; and it is his putter for which the Oxford and Cambridge Golfing Society do battle each January, the President's Putter. Hugh's great performance against Tait on that January day in 1894 makes this use of his putter all the more fitting.

When Freddie Tait was killed in action leading his men at Koodoosberg in February, 1900 he was only thirty; and Andrew Lang chose some lines from Wordsworth as his epitaph:

> The good die first,
> And those whose hearts are dry as summer dust
> Burn to the socket. [of the candlestick]

Let them suffice also for Hugh Kirkaldy, another whose death stunned the golfing world.

CHAPTER 11

J.H. TAYLOR'S FIRST
ST. ANDREWS OPEN: 1895

*I*N THE FOUR YEARS BEFORE THE CHAMPIONSHIP RETURNED TO ST. ANDREWS there were several important changes. Musselburgh with its nine holes had been quite a good test during almost twenty years since the Open had started going there every three years. But the Honourable Company of Edinburgh Golfers were only one of several Clubs who played at Musselburgh, and the wear and tear on the course became worse and worse the more that golf grew in popularity. Prestwick had had 18 holes since 1883, but although Musselburgh had tried desperately to emulate them, they had found it impossible to buy the extra land that they needed. So the Honourable Company decided to move to Muirfield and build 18 holes there. This had become imperative because it was clear that 36 holes in a day had become out of the question; with a 72-hole format, eight rounds on Musselburgh would have been deadly dull; and with the tremendous boom in golf, 18-hole courses – not least Sandwich and Hoylake – were available so that the Championship could be put on a broader basis.

Against the natural resistance of Musselburgh the Muirfield move was not easily achieved. They gathered as much prize money as possible and threatened to hold a rival tournament to coincide with the Open! Luckily for the Honourable Company, Musselburgh settled for a tournament earlier than the Championship, and another great Hoylake amateur, Harold H. Hilton, won the first 72-hole Open, at Muirfield. Significantly enough, John Ball Junior was second equal alongside Alex Herd, the 1902 Champion-to-be, and Hugh Kirkaldy. Hilton won again in 1897 at Hoylake.

1893 at Prestwick was Willie Auchterlonie's year; and the R&A were presented with his gold medal – the first real one – by Bea Auchterlonie, Laurie's widow, in 1988. They also have the seven clubs which were all that Willie ever used; and when I cleared out Laurie Auchterlonie's shop in June, 1988 shortly before his death I came upon a leather and canvas bag stamped 'W.A.' which Laurie confirmed was his father's – the only one he ever had between the 1890s and his death in 1962! 1893 saw the first Championship appearances of two immortals, John Henry Taylor and Harry Vardon.

1894 was important in at least two ways: Sandwich, the Royal St. George's Golf Club, staged the first Open on English soil; and J.H. Taylor recorded the first of his contribution of five Opens to the amazing total of sixteen wins recorded by Taylor, Vardon and Braid between 1894 and 1914. Until now Bob Martin with his victories in 1876 and 1885 had been the only double winner at St. Andrews, but from here on there would be three truly great Champions who each won twice in succession at St. Andrews: John Henry Taylor in 1895 and 1900, James Braid in 1905 and 1910, and Jack William Nicklaus in 1970 and 1978. That speaks volumes for the quality of the Old Course.

J. H. Taylor driving. His style was described as 'flat-footed' – ideal for the final round, 1895.

The two victories by Ball and Hilton in 1890 and 1892 had led to the introduction of a new event to conclude the proceedings at the 1894 Sandwich Open: a matchplay tournament with eight amateurs directly opposed to eight professionals in the first round. Tait did best, reaching the semi-final and losing to the eventual winner at the twentieth hole; but the professionals were too strong, and yet another fine player from Earlsferry, Douglas Rolland, beat Taylor in the final. Apart from Hilton's second Open in 1897 there were to be no further amateur triumphs until Robert Tyre Jones's three great wins culminating in the 1930 Grand Slam. It has remained like that ever since.

By 1895 when J.H. Taylor defended the Championship he had won at Sandwich the Scots were decidedly shaken. The previous year had shown that their traditional tee-shot, a low ball with a 'draw', was splendid at most holes on Scottish links; but at Sandwich a long carry was often needed from the tee, as also at Ganton and other fine English courses. Back at St. Andrews they knew every blade of grass – but that was not to prove enough.

John Henry Taylor is forever associated with Westward Ho! and the Royal North Devon Club. He himself said that he envied no golfer who had been raised in any place other than 'the nook in the West Country where there is Westward Ho! . . . which gave me principles and all my earliest and most valuable practice . . .' As a 'small, delicate boy with almost snow-white hair' (his own description) he 'played golf' with hedgerow sticks on Northam Burrows some time before he became a regular caddie on Saturday afternoons and after school. Of his first fee as a caddie – sixpence – he took home only half because his employer fined him 3d for losing a ball! Taylor gave this remarkable explanation: 'In those early days I was very short-sighted indeed and the player for whom I was caddying was not noted for his straight and accurate play.' Taylor had then gone as a gardener's boy for a while until, as Horace Hutchinson described it, 'the rushes of Westward Ho! links attracted him more than geraniums' and he became a greenkeeper instead. From his earliest days Taylor had played on a short course along with the other caddies and to the shortness of the holes, requiring only pitches from the tee, he ascribed his oft-acclaimed ability to play high stopping half-mashie shots to land by the pin. When asked about this favourite airborne route he used to reply in his usual rather clipped tones: 'There are no bunkers in the air'. His other main strength was his accurate driving in every conceivable condition. It was said of him that 'there were no hazards at Sandwich which he need regard save the direction flags'; invariably he was about a yard or so one side or the other, and once he hit one. Like Jamie Anderson, whom he had studied and admired when Taylor was only a lad of nine, he played very rapidly, wasting hardly any time on preliminaries. Like Willie Auchterlonie whose lifespan was very similar, Taylor was happy to use only seven clubs and go on splitting the fairways for as long as he could walk the course.

On Monday 10th June, just two days before the 1895 Open began, there was a very exciting preliminary.

Taylor and Andrew Kirkaldy played a 36-hole match for £50, and Andra won on the last green. As will be seen from the notice on page 56, crowd control was then in its infancy. Writing in November 1905, Taylor paid a very generous tribute to Andra. He had first played him in 1891 when Andra was at the height of his fame, having just defeated Willie Park Junior in their great match for £100 a-side. Taylor beat Kirkaldy on that first occasion and he now wrote:

> I have the most grateful memories of this match for another reason . . . It is because not only of the splendid way in which Andrew received his beating by a then unknown man, but on account of the extremely complimentary attitude that he assumed towards me . . . I have played with him many times since then, but I have no pleasanter memories than of that first match, and I honestly think that Andrew's words had a great and permanent effect upon me.

It is as well to show this other side of the coin; Kirkaldy's colourful but often coarse remarks have been unfortunately highlighted. This is how Taylor ended his tribute:

> The great crowd of golfers know him as a genial humorist of the links. I and others know him as one of the stoutest friends a man can have . . . a diamond of professional golf.

By 1895 10/- entry money was being charged and the prizes amounted to £100 to be divided as follows: 'First. £40 to the Winner of the Championship of which £10 shall be expended on a Gold Medal, and £30 given in money to a Professional, or in Plate to an Amateur Golfer. The Winner to have custody of the Championship Cup, but he must, if required, give security for its safe keeping.' (Earlier regulations had stated that the Cup would be lodged at the principal Club in the area where the winner resided.) Second, Third and Fourth prizes were £20, £10 and £7 respectively; the rest, from fifth to twelfth, totalled £23.

Sandy Herd started favourite because 'of his invincible play in tournaments since he had come north', and probably also because he was very good on fast greens. This time they were 'hard and ticklish in the extreme, sometimes almost white with hail, and again arid as ever in the strong sun'. Herd was paired with Andra Kirkaldy, and they made an excellent start, going round in 82 and 81 respectively.

Uncharacteristically, Taylor had an 86, falling foul of several bunkers on the way in. Ben Sayers, the little terrier from North Berwick, had been unlucky in cutting his hand on the rocks while bathing. This prompted Everard to write, 'had he foreseen such a calamity, by preference he would have fallen on his head'. In the circumstances he did well to come ninth. When Herd added a splendid 77 in the second round, and Taylor a 78, he was five shots ahead of him and Andrew Kirkaldy. The account of the Taylor/Kirkaldy match on the Monday had included these significant words: 'Taylor's putting did not come off on the hard greens . . .'

But now, on the evening of the first day's Championship play, heavy rain fell. Conditions for the second day were bright and bracing all morning, and Taylor, with an 80 to Herd's 82, came within three strokes of him at the start of the final round. Looking back, Herd would rue his six at the eleventh: with the stiff breeze against him his cleek shot poorly struck left him short of Strath bunker; he fluffed into it, and lay so badly that he had to play out backwards.

In the afternoon a strong east wind sprang up accompanied by lashing rain which forced strings of half-a-dozen spectators to huddle behind single umbrellas. Herd who was out early for the final round could not find the pace of the now sodden greens, was frequently short with his approaches and putts, and eventually slumped to an 85. To win, both Andrew Kirkaldy and George Fulford needed 77s, but very soon their challenge was over. Taylor could not succeed without an 81, and as he had put in an 80 on the previous, fine afternoon, it was not expected that he could touch it in the storm of wind and rain. His golf now was quite splendid. Let a Scot, William Proudfoot, describe Taylor's play:

> He handles every club with consummate ease and mastery . . . wastes no time . . . and drives a long sustained, straight skimmer in grand style. His approach mashie game is admirable and his putting with the patent cleek of the twisted neck is marvellously precise. I observed he was designated in a daily paper as a gamekeeper at Winchester, and I thought if his shooting was on a par with his golf, it would be rather rough on the partridges!

In this hour of extreme strain, with the odds still against him . . . and the honour of his country at stake Taylor never faltered, but played with a nerve and brilliancy that completely disarmed any hostile national sentiment there was and won the admiration of every genuine lover of the game. Squaring accounts with his Scots rival at the ninth hole, he held on his triumphant way, and before the home green was reached, it was plain that Open Championship honours were once more lost to Scotland. As he finished perfectly in

4 making a heroic 78 for the round, a ringing cheer from an ungrudging crowd hailed him victor and he was borne shoulder high from the scene of glorious strife – the first of his race to win the Open Championship on St. Andrews Links.' Apart from Dick Burton in 1939 he has also been the last.

As for Scotland, a native-born St. Andrean, Jock Hutchison, won in 1921 – but by then he was an American citizen.

Just a week after the Championship finished, a quite remarkable notice appeared:

NOTICE

At a Meeting of the Green Committee of St. Andrews Links held today, the following Resolution was unanimously come to, viz: 'That this Committee, learning that the golf holes on the Old Course have been filled up by the Custodian of the Links without authority, regret if any inconvenience should have been caused to the Public, and that such action should have been taken without notice and general agreement among golfers, but recognising that the Old Course is much in need of a rest resolve to allow the holes to remain closed until 30th June.'

ROBERT CATHCART, Convener.
JOHN McGREGOR, Provost.

ST. ANDREWS, 21st June, 1895.

This underlines what I said at the very start: the distinguishing feature of golf is the hole. Without it the game is literally aimless.

NOTICE.

THE COMMITTEE of the ROYAL AND ANCIENT GOLF CLUB appeal to all Golfers to assist them in the preservation of the Links,—

1. By always putting back and pressing down pieces of turf which they may cut out when playing with Irons or other clubs.

2. By teeing their balls only at the places marked out from time to time for the purpose.

If these suggestions are generally carried out, the Green will be in a better state than has been the case for years past, and the chances of getting "bad lies" and "cupped balls" will be greatly diminished.

J. WHYTE MELVILLE,
Chairman of Committee.

ST. ANDREWS, May, 1877.   J. COOK & SON, PRINTERS.

CHAPTER 12

ST. ANDREWS AGAIN: TAYLOR, 1900

*I*N 1895 THE UNITED STATES GOLF ASSOCIATION HAD BEEN FORMED, and in that year the first U.S. Open and Amateur Championships were contested. The first U.S. Amateur Champion, Charles Blair Macdonald, provides a link between British and American golf from the time of that first Open at St. Andrews in 1873 until his death in 1939. As a student at St. Andrews he had played in foursomes against Young Tommy Morris; he became the first American member of the R&A in February, 1894; and when in 1897 the R&A became the supreme authority on the Rules, except in the United States and nowadays Mexico, Macdonald was co-opted onto their Rules of Golf Committee to mediate in all matters concerning the U.S.G.A. His fine book published in 1928 has a good title: *Scotland's Gift – Golf.*

But after Taylor's victory in 1895, the Scots were reeling; and the Opens won by Hugh Kirkaldy and Willie Auchterlonie in 1891 and 1893 were to be our only ones during the last decade of the nineteenth century. Between 1896 and 1900 Vardon, Hilton and Taylor carried off the honours – Vardon on three occasions.

Son of Philippe Vardon, a Jersey gardener, Harry Vardon brought the Channel Islands into the news. In 1878 a golf course had been laid out on Grouville Common, Jersey, and young Harry and other village boys became interested in the game, playing with home-made clubs – as was John Henry Taylor at that time – and large white marbles. Aged 20, Vardon left the island to become a greenkeeper at Harrogate and a year later was Pro at the Bury Club. At 24 he had finished fifth equal in the 1894 Sandwich Open. Now, in 1896 he was Pro at Ganton and about to win the Open at Muirfield; but only after denying Taylor his third consecutive victory, in a play-off. The climax of the final round saw Vardon with a four to win and a five to tie with that desperately difficult second shot to the eighteenth to come. (I can see Player in that greenside bunker yet, on his way to winning the 1959 Championship.) Vardon played safe and got the necessary five. In the play-off Taylor had to get a three at the last, and hope that Vardon might take six. He went for the green, found the bunker that Vardon had dreaded, and himself took six.

There were two amateur favourites for the 1897 Championship at Hoylake: John Ball Junior and Harold Hilton, Open Champions both, who had learnt their golf there. For once, Ball's play during the last two rounds was catastrophic, 87 and 88, leaving him twenty shots behind Hilton. James Braid, the last of the Triumvirate to start winning the Open, came very close to doing so in 1897. After two excellent rounds Braid and Hilton were leading the field with totals of 154 and 155 respectively. But in the third round both seemed determined to throw it away; Braid took 82, Hilton 84 – and Hilton's summing up was 'weak-kneed golf'. Starting three shots behind Braid, Hilton then produced a quite splendid 75, putting a great

James Braid at the finish of his drive. He was the last of the Triumvirate–Taylor, Braid and Vardon to start winning the Open.

Harold Hilton, the great amateur and Open Champion 1892, 1897, at the top of his swing for a half-brassey approach.

second not very far from the hole at the last. His description of what followed is delightfully frank:

> Putt number one was not at all a bold one. One spectator called it a drunken effort and he was not far wrong. Putt number two dobbled about; and eventually made its entry into the hole at the back door, but it got there, and that was everything. I can see that ball now hesitating on the lip of the hole like a helpless derelict.

Braid had a three to tie and his second was very fine – never off the pin – but it ran six to eight yards past, and the putt slipped narrowly by.

In 1898 at Prestwick, Vardon was to win again, but only after a great battle with Willie Park Junior. Park, Champion in 1887 and 1889, was famous for one particular statement: 'The man who can putt is a match for anybody'. He had started the final round three shots ahead of Vardon who was playing a hole in front of him; but at the last he needed a three to tie and force a play-off. His drive was on the corner of the green and as Park was renowned for his putting, a tie seemed likely. His long putt was only a yard from the hole. The crowd pressing round elbowed Vardon out; he could see nothing, but after what seemed an eternity he heard a disappointed 'O-o-oh!'

At Sandwich in 1899, Vardon was at the top of his form and won easily. His brassie shots to the green were especially accurate; never far from the hole, they were a major factor in his victory. Some abnormal carries from the tee were always needed at Sandwich, and Vardon was one of the few who could achieve them when a fresh easterly breeze sprang up on the closing day. Indeed, several competitors complained that many of the carries were unfair. The feature of Vardon's scoring was that he played magnificent golf, especially in the first half of his second and third rounds, then quite clearly 'sat on' his lead. Many felt that he could have won by more than five shots had he chosen. As it was, he totalled 310, Jack White was on 315, Kirkaldy on 319 and Taylor on 320. Perhaps the best measure of Vardon's brilliance is that his aggregate was no fewer than sixteen strokes less than Taylor's on this same course when winning in 1894.

In September 1899, Frederick Guthrie Tait duly won the Autumn Meeting of the R&A and soon afterwards set sail for South Africa and the Boer War. By December he had been shot through the thigh in the Battle of Magersfontein, and was convalescing in a hospital near Cape

The imperturbable Vardon gets away a fine tee shot at Cruden Bay despite the attentions of a fox terrier. He is watched by J. H. Taylor. Dogs were banned for the first time at the 1900 St. Andrews Open.

Vardon driving . . . this time without the dog. D. C. Thomson & Co. Ltd., Dundee.

Town. He wrote to a friend that he healed easily and would soon return to the Front. By early February, 1900 he had become a Scottish national hero, killed in action at the head of his men. He was only thirty, of an age with Vardon, Taylor and Braid, and from his performances till then would have been in fierce contention with them and others until at least the outbreak of World War I in 1914. It does not seem to have been noted that, apart from Vardon, he had a better average Open Championship position from 1896 to 1899 than anyone else: 3=, 3=, 5, 7=. In addition he had been Amateur Champion in 1896 and 1898, and lost to Ball only at the 37th hole in 1899.

The Open Championship of 1900 at St. Andrews coincided with celebrations of a victory in South Africa: the stronghold of Kruger, the President of the Transvaal, had been surrendered and 4,000 soldier-prisoners set free. 'The old grey city by the sea' had lost its greyness and coldness and was bright with bunting in every street and square. Old Tom's workmen had made an effigy of Kruger soaked in pitch which was duly burned at the Mercat Cross. Soon too there would be new bunkers at the ninth hole on the Old Course, 'Mr Kruger' and 'Mrs Kruger', so-called it was explained because of 'their hidden and treacherous nature'!

Before the 1900 Championship began, one special rule framed for the occasion, and strictly enforced, is worth noting: no dogs were to be allowed on the course on any pretext whatsoever. The Championship Committee must soon have been very pleased with their decision because, when the draw brought the Open and the Amateur Champions out of the hat, Vardon and Hilton, there were problems enough in controlling the crowds without having dogs running around. Other favourites – Taylor, Herd, White and Braid – had small galleries; but Andra Kirkaldy, the local hero, had none. Vardon said later that a well-regulated crowd is not a hindrance but an inspiration, although at St. Andrews that day he found the crowd very disconcerting as they got in line of the stroke. This was also Hilton's experience. After a magnificent outward nine of 36, he took 47 to come back. Vardon and Taylor both took 79 for the first round. In the end Vardon would lose by eight shots, and he put it all down to his poor putting. He was not long back from America, where, as he said, 'the greens are as hard as

Vardon Putting.

cement, and that rather upsets the putting on the greens here, which are not so like macadamized roads'. In general, American tours of 20,000 miles are reckoned to have damaged Vardon's health. He had several visits to sanatoria, notably one in 1902.

In fairness to Taylor it has to be said that his golf in the 1900 Open was every bit as dominating as Vardon's had been in 1899 at Sandwich. He broke 80 in all four rounds, finishing with a splendid 75. His 77 on the first afternoon was achieved on bumpy, hard greens – and we know that he preferred softer ones. He did not need much luck, but he must have been delighted on the morning of the second day: an easterly drizzle helped to soften the putting greens and make them true. There would be many in the crowds who knew that his earlier 77 equalled one first made by Young Tommy Morris in tournament play, as well as Herd's in 1895. Taylor's 75 in the final round with a gutta ball stands unparalleled in the history of golf. His 309 won by eight shots from Vardon, thirteen from Braid and fourteen from Jack White. Detailed scores for these four are available, and they reveal how remarkably difficult the seventeenth hole was before the arrival of the core-wound ball with its cover allowed the players to get much nearer the green in two. Between them they played the hole sixteen times. Vardon and White took six throughout; Braid managed two fives, and Taylor had one – thanks to a seven-yard putt!

Taylor was more durable than either Vardon or Braid, whose failing eyesight prevented him from adding to the five Opens he had won by 1910. 'J.H.', when faced with problems, violent weather or exciting finishes, just pulled his cap one little bit tighter down his massive forehead. It was in this mood in 1924 at Hoylake, when Walter Hagen won, that Taylor aged 53 finished fifth just six strokes behind. Had the qualifying rounds been added to the championship play he would have beaten the world by several strokes.

He certainly won 'high honours' in 1900 at St. Andrews, and, although the verse is far from sparkling, these lines convey the general pleasure felt at his second St. Andrews victory:

> From the old university town
> Looking out on the cold North Sea,
> He carried high honours down
> To his home in the south countree.

CHAPTER 13

BRAID'S GREAT YEARS: 1901 TO 1910

*B*Y 1901 IT HAD SEEMED THAT THE COMBINATION OF TAYLOR AND VARDON would continue to dominate golf in the British Isles. The last Scottish victory had been Willie Auchterlonie's in 1893; but just as there had been only two Scots winning the Open in the 1890s, so there were only two Englishmen between 1901 and 1910: Vardon won his fourth championship in 1903; Taylor added his fourth in 1909. For the rest there were seven Scottish victories, and the first-ever win recorded by a foreigner, the Frenchman, Arnaud Massy, in 1907. Braid won five of these Opens and his record during that time can be compared only with Tom Watson's five Opens between 1975 and 1983.

The comparative decline in Vardon's play during the early twentieth century was partly due to his exhausting American tours: a programme of playing, travelling, giving exhibitions and instructional displays. But Browning tells us that Vardon went at the age of twelve for several years to work on a dairy farm. In the 1880s the sterilisation of milk by heating was in its infancy, and there were no tuberculin-tested cows, so that untreated milk carried a serious

Braid starting the final round, 1901.

threat. Whether or not Vardon became a victim in that way, he certainly had to be treated for lung trouble, and over the years spent many months in various sanatoria. There is no suggestion that Taylor was in poor health during Braid's great years, years when he dominated the golf scene and at times seemed quite unbeatable.

When James Braid won his first Open, at Muirfield in 1901, the gutta ball was still supreme in Britain, even although an American, Coburn Haskell, had patented the first core-wound ball with a cover in April, 1899, and it was then in use in the States. Indeed, Taylor had had an opportunity to try the Haskell out in 1900 at Wheaton near Chicago soon after he had won the St. Andrews Open and was touring America with Vardon. Haskell sent Taylor a box of balls with the request that he would give this 'entirely revolutionary type' a trial. He did play a few shots with one, but decided that it would be too great a gamble to switch to the Haskell just before the American Championship. Darwin tells us that this was a decision 'he has ever since regretted'. By the time of the 1901 Open at Muirfield no one had as yet a supply of Haskells, and that allowed Braid to reap the full benefit of his extra length with the gutta.

He was thirty-one at this time, after enjoying a distinguished career as an artisan amateur while following his trade as a joiner. Then he took up clubmaking, and so entered the professional ranks. His enormous power was amusingly demonstrated when he partnered a long-handicap lady in a mixed foursome. (It was an Edwardian misogynist who called it a 'forced mix'em!'.) She put their ball in a small gorse bush. Braid moved it and much of the bush about twenty-five yards whereupon his partner exclaimed, 'Oh, I'm glad you can mis-hit them too, Mr Braid!'

As early as 1897, A.J. Robertson, the Editor of *Golf*, pinpointed the main features of Braid's game, and approach to the game, which would make him a champion: 'Even when the prospect looks most dark he plays to the end with dogged determination ... Genial imperturbability is the keynote of his character . . . There are two other qualities in Braid – a judicious compounding of caution and brilliant dash.' These were the themes that golf writers echoed from that point until Braid achieved his fifth and last Open in 1910.

Just before the 1901 Championship at Muirfield Braid had won a very impressive victory at Musselburgh and now started firm favourite. His length on occasion brought him figures which others could not match. One outstanding example was in the second round at the long fifth which others found unreachable in two; Braid with a wonderful second to two yards had an eagle three – although it was not called that then. After 36 holes he was seven shots ahead of Taylor. Vardon did better, tying with Braid at that point; but, ominously, Vardon had lost a four-stroke lead built up after 27 holes. It looked very much like a two-horse race. On that second day successive trains brought enormous crowds all eager to see the great tussle between Braid and Vardon. They reckoned that there were 4,000 spectators on the course, and their interest, excitement and general fine feeling were in evidence throughout. Tom Vardon, who was well down the field, decided to retire, and caddy for his brother. As Harry Vardon was drawn with Taylor, the Open Champion, they took a huge gallery with them. But Vardon was far below his usual form, spraying his tee shots, and, even with some wonderful recoveries, he dropped strokes here and there. Braid was on form from the start, and his 74, equalled by Taylor, put him five shots ahead of Vardon. In the final round Braid played with extreme caution and returned a useful 80. At the very end of that round there was a touch of drama. Braid described it thus: 'With the very last shot that I played to reach the green I broke my

Sandy Herd, Open Champion, 1902.

cleek. I came down hard on a little piece of turf sticking up behind the ball, and away went the head of the club and a piece of shaft with it . . . Thank goodness I got my shot in just the same, and the ball ran up nicely on the green.' The door was slightly open, and in fact Vardon eventually needed three fours to tie with Braid. His task became nearly hopeless when at the sixteenth he topped into a bunker and took six. Far from getting two threes now, Vardon finished four, five and Braid was home by three shots; Taylor finished just one stroke further back. To his great credit Harold Hilton squeezed in behind the three great professionals, in a tie with Jack White. Laidlay was next, on his home course. His grandson, David Stobart, tells a lovely story about Laidlay's taking out his rowing boat, lifting his lobster pots, coming home and then walking to Muirfield from his home, Invereil, at North Berwick, to play in a championship – perhaps this one.

Before the 1902 Championship at Hoylake, Harold Hilton infuriated the Scottish public when he wrote that there was some 'decadence' in Sandy Herd's game. Perhaps it had fallen

Willie Auchterlonie and Sandy Herd, staunch friends and opponents, forty years on, with the Swilcan Burn behind. St. Andrews University, Cowie Collection.

away a little at the end of the gutta era; but now Sandy was to switch to the Haskell at the last minute after damning it with faint praise just a few days before. The evidence in favour of the Haskell had been seen at the Amateur Championship played a little earlier – and at Hoylake at that. Both the finalists, the great all-rounder, S.H. Fry, and Charles Hutchings from the home Club, Royal Liverpool, were using Haskells, and as Hutchings was then fifty-three it was felt that the ball might have had something to do with his victory. Bernard Darwin recalled that when he was on the way to Hoylake for that championship he was asked by a friend whether he would use the Haskell ball and had replied, 'What is that?' On arrival he found that a few players had managed to get a supply of the new balls – but 'no more were to be had for love or money'. However, Herd was playing a practice round for the Open at Hoylake with John Ball when the great amateur gave him a Haskell with which to try some shots. Herd was greatly impressed. He had wondered why Ball was outdriving him so easily when he had normally had the edge. Now he knew the answer, and decided to play the Haskell, in the Open. It took considerable courage. He had little time to get used to its feeling of lightness off the club, and its variable performance when fairways were hard. But that was more than balanced by the extra twenty or thirty yards it gave, and the fact that a poorly hit shot – severely penalised by a gutty – escaped as if it had been better struck. Like Young Tommy, Herd was immediately recognisable by the number of waggles he took before striking the ball. No doubt like Young Tommy he would find his shafts breaking just below his right hand because of eventual hickory fatigue.

In the 1902 championship it was Harry Vardon who produced a very fine first round of 72 which gave him the lead by at least four shots from the rest. The opening comment about Vardon's round is rather bewildering: 'At the first hole he drove twice out of bounds but, nevertheless secured a six.' Rule 31 in 1902 stated: 'If a ball be driven out of bounds, a ball shall be dropped at the spot from which the stroke was played, under penalty of loss of the distance.' To get a six nowadays the competitor would need to hole a medium iron shot! But Vardon's play, with a gutta ball, was brilliant with four threes in an outward half of 35, followed by a very fine inward nine of 37, finishing with two fours. His 77 in the second round allowed Ray, Herd, Braid and Hilton to draw a little nearer, but he still had a four-shot lead. Who could possibly bridge that gap? In the third round, Herd managed a fine 73; Vardon, however, was putting so badly that he took 80, and the loss of seven shots to Herd left the Scot three ahead. Braid and Taylor were a massive eight strokes behind Herd going into the final round. He finished weakly with an 81, but it was just good enough. Vardon eventually had two fours to tie, and achieved the first of them beautifully. He had a fine tee shot at the last, and a play-off seemed inevitable. But he only half-hit his approach – it was no more than that – left himself twenty yards from the flag, and had been lucky to jump a bunker in so doing. No doubt shaken by it all, he overran the hole by two yards, missed the return, and barring miracles Herd was home. Braid, and Robert Maxwell, twice Amateur Champion, managed 74s but that was not quite good enough. From then on the gutta ball was doomed, even although for over fifty years it had been dependable, giving the best results to the best players.

For all Braid's brilliance during this decade, Vardon had now been second three years running. Next year at Prestwick in 1903, he won his fourth championship, even although he had been advised to avoid the stress of the Open; his health had again deteriorated. There was a record entry, so that play began at an unprecedented 8.30, and at a modest estimate 6,000 people were present on the second day. For the first time it was reported that the click of a camera had upset a player – Vardon, no less, after he had placed a splendid mashie shot a yard from the pin at the thirteenth in the third round. 'Here the attentions of a photographic assassin who fired his dastardly shot while the player was engaged and then fled with his prize probably accounted for the missing of the putt ...' But Vardon had three fine rounds in succession: 73, 77, 72, and led comfortably from start to finish, even although he had to struggle against exhaustion during the final round, yet achieved a 78. His nearest challenger after two rounds was A.H. Scott whose little clubmaking factory now stands derelict alongside the fourth fairway at Earlsferry, no longer bearing the proud sign 'A.H. SCOTT, CLUBMAKER TO KING GEORGE THE FIFTH'. His son, David, was still exporting fine clubs to America in the 1950s. In the end Vardon won by six shots from his brother, Tom, with Jack White, Sandy Herd and James Braid in rapid succession after that, but several shots further back. Scott was a very creditable sixth equal, two shots ahead of John Henry Taylor. Harry Vardon's next win would not be till 1911; but who can say what might have been his eventual tally had his health been more stable in the intervening years?

In 1904 at Sandwich the record entry of 144 led to the introduction of a third day's play: one round on Wednesday and Thursday, and two on Friday, a format which was retained until 1966. It was also in 1904 that the full impact of the Haskell on the game of golf was felt for the first time, and a very worthy champion, Jack White, fulfilled the promise indicated by his performance in previous years. This is a brief account of what he wrote soon after that victory:

> I was born at Pefferside, East Lothian, August 15, 1873, and as a boy of ten I began carrying clubs on Saturdays at North Berwick. The game took my fancy after seeing such players as Willie Campbell and Sayers playing. During this time I caddied for Mr J.E. Laidlay when he won his first Amateur in 1889, and travelled to places like Hoylake with him. My game was fairly good, and when Mr Laidlay gave me a round now and again I found I could very nearly hold my own. Golf was not a very rosy profession then, but I felt it was worth my while to stick to golf.

White was in the prize list – never a very long one in those days – as early as 1897 and 1898. For twenty-five years he was at Sunningdale and built up a fine reputation as a clubmaker, the craft he had learnt from working in Tom Dunn's shop for a few months after he left school. He it was who, in 1911, used a special facing of catgut on drivers, having found that he could hit a golf ball with a racket a very long way. His invention gave Sunningdale golfers an extra twenty yards, and perhaps led to the ban on insets in the face of clubs.

A few brief statistics will illustrate the Haskell's impact: the championship record at Sandwich was first reduced from 75 to 71, then to 69 and finally to 68. But with a strong north-east wind blowing on the first day and without much rain for a week, the greens were very keen – 'Players were . . . almost afraid to touch the ball . . . they were not able to hit it firmly enough to keep the straight line ...' – and also the wind was moving the ball off course. Not unnaturally, no one managed better than a 75. Sherlock of Oxford had a 71 the following day, but at the halfway stage Harry Vardon led by two shots, and by six from Jack White, a lead which would have been unassailable a few years before. The final day was perfect for golf; overnight rain had done wonders for the greens.

In the third round James Braid broke 70, the first one to do so in any Open championship. It all sounds so modern – but it was 1904:

'Excited Scouts hurried to where spectators were assembled with the news that the big Scotsman was out in the astounding score of 31: five 3s and four 4s.' He dropped a stroke at the sixteenth, but his 69 was loudly acclaimed. Jack White with an excellent 72 had moved one ahead of Vardon but was relegated by Braid's phenomenal score to second place. Tom Vardon on his home course, and Taylor came next, followed by that very fine amateur Jack Graham Junior, who some ten years later was killed in action in the First World War.

In the final round it was a desperately close-run thing. White was off early and played like a champion from the start; a two at the 240-yard 5th against the breeze helped him to be two over threes for the first six holes! After that whenever he went over par he at once followed with a birdie – the mark of great golfers in any age. His 69 equalled Braid's record and gave him a total of 296; he was considered practically a safe winner. Braid made a bold dash for a second championship. Out in 34, he needed a three and two fours to tie with White. A spectator told him that White had taken 70, Braid played cautiously for three fours, and was very upset when he lost by a shot. At the eighteenth he needed a three to tie, and with a 270-yard drive he needed only a pitch near the hole – but he was several yards past and missed the return. That was not the end of the excitement. Taylor needed a 67 to tie, and as that was considered impossible, enterprising Pressmen had sent away White's name as winner long before the finish. There seemed no risk, but at about the time when people were opening their evening papers to read the news, Taylor had his big chance to tie. In the end he failed by one shot and the ball with which he made that record 68 is in the Trophy Room of the Royal and Ancient.

The 1905 Amateur Championship. Mr Barry driving at the 18th tee – his style was all his own.

When the Open returned to St. Andrews in 1905 it was clear that the Green Committee had taken steps to avoid any repetition of the record-breaking scores at Sandwich. Little pot bunkers had been introduced just big enough in that fine modern phrase 'for an angry man and his sand-iron'. In normal conditions good golfers will blame themselves if they are trapped in this way; but here, with a record entry of 152 and three days' play, conditions varied considerably depending on the luck of the draw for starting times, and avoiding bunkers was at times a matter of luck too. The comparison with several recent Opens is perhaps too obvious to mention. Old Tom, now very old and frail, was acting as a starter for the last time. On that first day, Wednesday June 7, 1905, at St. Andrews 'a high cold wind blew from the north-east, and as it increased in force as the day wore on, those who were far down the list had much the worst of the luck'. Add to that the fact that the greens were so treacherously keen as to be termed 'skating rinks' by some competitors, and it is no wonder that no one broke eighty. At that figure Taylor, Harry Vardon and Herd were bracketed, with Braid a stroke further back. But there was no comparison between the conditions faced by Taylor and Herd who were off early, by Braid in the middle of the draw, and by Vardon who was far down the list. Taylor finished 7, 5 and threw away the chance of a good lead; Braid was bunkered again and again but recovered splendidly. He was 'in the field at the fourteenth and yet got a four', so there was no out of bounds there then. He was greatly helped in his putting throughout this Championship by his recent study of hard greens which had led him to take his aluminium putter for his approach putts, but change to the putting cleek for the short ones. What a splendid 80 Vardon must have had; but his subsequent play was probably affected by

Harry Vardon's bunker shot at the 13th in the third round of the 1905 Open.

the effort required. The only amateur to keep within fifteen shots of the leader after 36 holes and so qualify for the two rounds on Friday was Jack Graham Junior, whose 83 with a seven at the seventeenth was very fine considering that he was quite a late starter. Poor Barry, the 1905 Amateur Champion, a St. Andrews student, was second last out, and took 50 to come home, for his 90. His style was all his own.

For Thursday's play the weather had improved, but a strong easterly wind was blowing, and scores were not noticeably better. Indeed, Taylor had a wretched day, taking five shots more than on the Wednesday, and with a similarly weak finish. Sixes at both the sixteenth and seventeenth may have unnerved him: anyway, he struck the Swilcan Bridge with his final drive, and a five took him to 85. When Braid managed a 78, coming home in an almost perfect 38, it seemed that he would head the qualifiers for the last two rounds; but Rowland Jones' 77 just pushed him into second place. When Harry Vardon went out in the afternoon he took such a large gallery 'that the rope had to be brought into use for the first time at the meeting'. He was twice bunkered on the way out, but 39 was a perfectly good score. He lost several shots on the greens coming home, and then at the eighteenth he produced a most extraordinary shot – one of his 'specialities' as he jokingly said. In playing his second shot Vardon got the ball up to a great height and there was so much slice on it that it curled right round to the houses overlooking the green and bounced off the top of the bay window of an upper room on to the roof of a four-storey building! As the penalty was only distance he escaped with a five, and an 82, still well in contention. There was a difference of only seven strokes in the scores of the top fifteen qualifiers; and since these included Braid, Taylor, Vardon, Herd and Willie Park, it was felt that over 36 holes any one of them might produce the necessary golf although Braid was looking more and more like a winner. Many looked to Taylor who, although seven shots behind, had won the last two St. Andrews Opens; but conditions did not favour his high, normally stopping, mashie shots – a pitch and run was needed.

For the final two rounds on the Friday there was only a slight breeze. The leader, Rowland Jones, was first off, but after a steady start he went 8, 6 at the fifth and sixth, and never recovered from that. An 87 was far too many. Taylor with a 78 made up all seven shots and more upon Jones, but he had made no impression on Braid's six-shot lead over him. The Scot had gone out in 36, demonstrating his tremendous power by reaching the long fifth in two, after terrific wooden club play, for a fine four. Needing 5, 4 to tie with Taylor's third-round score, he managed a five with much difficulty at the seventeenth – the 'death-trap' as *Golf Illustrated* described it – but luck was with him at the last hole. He pulled his second which seemed destined for the Clubhouse steps when it was stopped by the crowd, and two putts gave him a four. Harry Vardon was much troubled by the glassy greens, and took 84, nine shots behind Braid.

In the final round Braid was a prime favourite, some 4,000 spectators attending him. When he was out in 38, again reaching the long fifth in two, but this time three-putting, it seemed to be all over. He started back well, the highlights being two long shots to the edge of the big thirteenth green, and a four, followed by three perfect shots at the long fourteenth, and stone dead for a five. He had now reached a point where it was possible to get into dreadful trouble. The rules as revised in September 1904 now included the local one:

'The grass within the railway fence, the grass bounding the roads at the Corner of the Dyke and at the seventeenth hole, shall not be considered hazards.' Elsewhere you could go

Braid's railway shot at the 16th in the final round of the 1905 Open.

out of bounds, as we have seen, for the loss of distance only. Let Braid tell us what happened to him as he played alongside the railway fence at the fifteenth and sixteenth holes:

> Going to the fifteenth I sliced my second shot on to the railway. Playing off it I hit a man, and the ball rebounded from him and went to a nasty place where it was tucked up against a bush. The hole cost me six strokes and though this was the loss of a couple, I was still according to my reckoning in a very comfortable position. But at the next hole the case began to look rather serious, and it was very fortunate that I had made my position so strong early in the round, or that hole would probably have been fatal to my prospects. From the tee I drove right over the Principal's Nose and pitched into the bunker beyond. I was lying rather well, with the result that I became too venturesome and attempted to put the ball on the green instead of settling for a five . . . I got it on to the railway and . . . found it lying in a horrible place, tucked up against one of the iron chairs in which the rails rest . . . I took my niblick and tried to hook it out but did not succeed, the ball moving only a few yards, and being in much the same position against the rail. With my fourth I got it back on to the course but . . . it went some thirty yards past the hole near to the bunker on the left of the second green. As the ground was I had only about a yard to come and go on with a run-up shot . . . a bold and very risky shot to play; but . . . it came off, the ball running dead, so that I got my six.

1905: a rush for the last green over the Swilcan bridge.

Braid felt that in all four rounds that was the best shot that he played when everything depended on it. He also felt that it had been 'injudicious' not to take a two-shot penalty by lifting his ball away from the rail when he arrived there in two. He finished 5, 4, and won by five shots from Taylor and Jones. It was a very short prize list – only six in all – and it was a new experience for Harry Vardon not to find a place on that list.

One main factor in Braid's victory was his splendid play at the long fifth, fourteenth and seventeenth. Full scores were given for the first three, and their totals for these twelve holes played were as follows:

Braid: 5, 5, 4, 5; 4, 5, 6, 5; 5, 5, 5, 5 = 59
Taylor: 5, 5, 5, 5; 6, 6, 5, 5; 7, 6, 5, 5 = 65
Jones: 5, 5, 8, 5; 7, 5, 6, 5; 4, 5, 6, 5 = 66

Braid's victory was received very much as Taylor's had been in 1900: '. . . immediately the stalwart Scotsman had holed out his last putt he was surrounded by a surging crowd and lifted shoulder high, while hundreds of hands were held out to grasp his . . .'

In 1906 at Muirfield, the problem of far too many entries for the Championship was as bad as ever. As one report put it, '. . . things have come to such a pass because of the vaingloriousness of second-rate professionals and amateurs who annually cumber the field . . .' This was the third year now that three days were needed, and on the Wednesday and Thursday a nine o'clock start still meant that the last couple were not back until eight o'clock at night. The luck of the draw went against James Braid; he was off at five o'clock on both days. As he said himself, he made the mistake the first day of going down to the course too early, and the hanging about did him no good at all. On the second day he kept away from the course until it was nearly time to start, having played a quiet round in a foursome on a nearby course just to keep his hand and eye in. After the first 36 holes, Braid was four shots behind the leader, John Henry Taylor, and three behind Harry Vardon and Jack Graham Junior; all three had been off between 9 and 10 a.m. on both Wednesday and Thursday. A modern-day defending champion would almost certainly have more to say than Braid did when sent out twice after there had already been eight hours' continuous play to unchanged pin positions. The highlight of the play so far had been Taylor's recovery in the second round from an indifferent 41 out because of poor putting. He then came back in 31 for a 72. The rule eliminating those who were fifteen shots off the pace had reduced the field to 72 for the two rounds on the Friday.

Rowland Jones, who had come second equal with Taylor in 1905, had on that occasion thrown his chance away in the third round with a horrible 87. In 1906 he had been off even later than Braid on the first two days so that his total, one shot better than Braid's was highly creditable. His 73 in the third round was the best score returned, and going into the final round he was tied with Taylor on 225, Braid and Vardon were on 227, Graham on 228. No one else was really in contention; but Arnaud Massy, the champion in 1907, played himself into the prize list with a 78, and came sixth. Poor Jones had a sad 83 in the final round and dropped to fifth place. Taylor was throwing away his chance at the same time. He in fact needed a spectacular final hole to get round in 80. He pulled into the rough and from there played a brilliant brassie, his ball almost finding the hole. From his first two holes in the Championship, Vardon had dropped four shots to Braid, Taylor and Graham. They had all started 3, 4; Vardon required four putts on the first green, missing from less than a foot, and he then took six at the second with a skied drive and a bunkered second. In the end he was third, five shots behind Braid. For once again James Braid had played splendid golf just when it was needed. He needed a 76 – not by any means an easy target – and he achieved a 73.

> *Golf Illustrated* summed it up thus: 'It becomes evident that another feature of the meeting and one none the less interesting because it was so utterly lacking in novelty, was that despite their tardiness in getting on to their best game, the old "triumvirate" once again had the championship entirely to themselves at the finish . . .' It was to be a different story in 1907.

Perhaps because Braid and Rowland Jones had been off so late on both the Tuesday and the Wednesday at Muirfield, the Royal Liverpool Club decided that at Hoylake in 1907 they would find a better way of arranging the qualifying rounds:

> On Tuesday and Wednesday in the Championship week, entrants will qualify to play for the championship by two rounds on each day – one-half of the entrants to be drawn to play on the Tuesday and the remainder on the Wednesday. The thirty players returning the lowest scores on each day, including all who may tie, will be qualified to play. On Thursday and Friday the championship will be played for by such entrants as may have qualified under the rules at present governing it.

At first sight this seems to be an improvement; but in fact it meant that those who played their 36 holes on the Tuesday then had a rest day, while the other half played two rounds on the Wednesday and – if they qualified – played, in all, six rounds in three days! Those who played on the Tuesday included the ultimate winner Arnaud Massy, Sandy Herd and Rowland Jones. All the other big names played on the Wednesday: Taylor, Vardon, Braid, Jack Graham, George Duncan, Ted Ray and Willie Park Junior. What is more, as indicated by the fact that a score of 165 qualified on the Tuesday, but 170 on the Wednesday, conditions were far more

Arnaud Massy, 1907 Open Champion, driving, cheerful as ever.

testing for the Triumvirate and the others: a strong and gusty wind blew across the course from the west and as the day progressed the wind gathered strength. There was no recorded word of complaint at the time, but clearly there were mutterings later.

Before the Championship proper began on the Thursday, all the usual contenders were known to be in good form: Braid, the holder, was fancied for a fourth Championship; Harry Vardon, although he had lost to Braid in the professional International match, was playing as powerful a long game and almost as good a short game as ever; neither Herd nor Taylor had shown any falling away. But they all knew that Arnaud Massy, the Frenchman from Biarritz, had defeated the lot of them at Cannes that spring. Moreover, the weather promised to be stormy – and Massy had been trained to battle against howling Atlantic winds on the Biarritz course, where he had also caddied for some years for British golfers who went there in the winter months. He displayed a remarkable aptitude for the game and was brought to North

Berwick by Everard Hambro where he further developed his talents under Ben Sayers. Massy had been playing left-handed because these had been the only available clubs; but Sayers altered this, and his progress became even more marked. His temperament and his physique were both first-class. Bernard Darwin said of him: 'Massy has a fine swashbuckling air and a cheerful chuckling way with him that is most engaging.'

Statistics can be very misleading, but it is perhaps worth mentioning that after their two tough qualifying rounds on the Wednesday, only three of those from first to tenth equal on the Thursday had not enjoyed a rest the previous day. Braid was a full ten shots off the pace, but as he explained – not at the time – 'The fact was that I was not feeling very fit, and this was accentuated by the perfectly shocking weather that prevailed'. 'J.H.', the old warhorse, was just a shot behind Massy after 36 holes, George Duncan was four, and Harry Vardon was eight. Two local players, Tom Ball and George Pulford, were one and two shots respectively behind Massy; but on the final day Massy was too good to be caught. True, in the third round Taylor had had two halfs of 38 – and Massy had taken 42 to the turn. However, he came back in 36 and was only a shot behind Taylor before the afternoon round. Braid and Vardon had good scores, but they were by now out of the reckoning. Massy was out an hour and twenty minutes after Taylor, and when Taylor took 80 Massy knew that he needed a 78. One report said, 'Massy was just the man to go out and perform a definite task set before him'. His 77 meant he had won with a stroke to spare.

Massy had married a North Berwick girl and when his daughter was born soon after the 1907 Open, he had her christened 'Hoylake', in the same way that James Braid had had a son christened Harry Muirfield Braid.

For the 1908 Open at Prestwick it was clear that the qualifying rounds would have to be arranged so that no successful competitor would be called upon to play six rounds in three days as a reward for his achievement! This time the field was divided into two sections as before; but the first section played one round on Tuesday morning and a second on Wednesday afternoon, and the other played on Tuesday afternoon and Wednesday morning, an arrangement which made it as fair as possible for everybody.

Of the five championships won by James Braid during this decade, his 1908 win was especially decisive. Throughout the Championship proper, the weather was very good, and this was reflected in some remarkably low scoring. Harry Vardon's record 72 when winning at Prestwick in 1903 was beaten three times besides three ties. In the first round Braid had a 70. That record lasted only fifty minutes before Ernest Gray turned up with a 68! Sandy Herd on being asked during his round of 74 how he was getting on, replied: 'Pretty well; I'm playing the game of gowf, not mad stuff like yon fellow who did 68.' Both Vardon and Taylor had played themselves right out of it after 36 holes, the former being 'very shaky both off the tee and on the green', the latter having gone 'all to pot with his putter'. Braid added a 72 to his 70, and his 142 put him fourteen and fifteen shots ahead of Taylor and Vardon respectively. Those closest to him were between five and seven shots off the pace. It was in his second round that Braid brought off the amazing recovery which is talked about yet: '. . . at the eighth he extricated himself, or rather his ball, from a whin bush by apparently taking the whole bush along with the ball on to the green – a tremendous effort.' In the third round, Braid made a terrible mess of the dreaded 'Cardinal', the third hole. Playing short of the bunker he sliced into the rough, and instead of coming out sideways tried brute force and managed to 'hoick' it into the sand close under the palisades. He seemed to lose his head, took an iron instead of his niblick, trying to get home with a slice, hit the sleepers and shot over the burn out of bounds. Then he tried again without coming out. The hole cost him an eight, and someone remarked, 'This is not going to be such a one-horse show after all'. But he reckoned without his man. Braid was thoroughly furious with himself – but the only effect on his game was to make him play better, and he salvaged a 77. For the final round an enormous crowd spread over the course, most of them to see Braid who still held a six-shot lead, but a few to follow Tom Ball who played splendid golf, young as he was, and his 74 made him runner-up. Braid accompanied by 'a running, raging, but withal well-behaved mob', probably never played better golf in his life.

His 72, 36 both ways, consisted of three 5s, three 3s and the rest 4s, an exhibition which, at that time at any rate, only he could provide. He ended up no fewer than eight strokes ahead of the field, and, looking very unhappy, was carried into the club enclosure. A reporter summed up: 'In fact, he is now in a class by himself – he drives further and putts better than any of the others, and they know it, and cheerfully acknowledge the fact.'

In 1909 the Championship went to Deal for the one and only time, to the Cinque Port Club, where their Championship Committee had to organise a field of 203 players. To their great credit they kept to a tight schedule and on the Tuesday soon after 7 p.m. the last couple, who had started just before five, came in. The second qualifying day went equally well, and the only notable casualty was Jack White the 1904 Champion who with rounds of 86 and 87 missed the cut by twelve shots – an amazingly poor performance for him.

Braid, of course, started firm favourite for the Championship proper, and as Harold Hilton pointed out, 'one never came upon a single person anxious to wager on the event' who found it possible to back Braid. 'Fortunately for them, "bookies" were conspicuous by their absence.'

But as it turned out Braid was more or less out of the running after the first two rounds; it was to be Taylor's turn again at long last. He had come very close on several occasions since his win at St. Andrews in 1900. This time he was an early starter, when he had only dullness and a fresh north-east wind to contend with; but soon after Braid and Duncan went out a little over an hour later, the rain began and the wind freshened. So Taylor had most of the bad weather for the last nine holes. He had gone out in 41, and must have then played splendidly to achieve a 74. As for James Braid, his troubles began as early as the second hole, and, as Harold Hilton put it, 'he may be said to have begun the process of burying his chance for the Championship there'. Not only did he take six, three putting from four yards, but for the time being it quite seemed to upset his usual fine temperament. 'Jimmy then did what I have never seen him do before – he chided some spectators for talking . . . The mere fact of his speaking left quite a feeling of awe and consternation amongst those present.' In all he had three 6s in his 80, while Duncan, a stroke worse than Braid on the way out, came back in 35 for a 77. It is possible that Duncan contributed to Braid's problems by his own speed of play. He didn't write *Golf at the Gallop* for nothing! James was 'slow and methodical', sometimes taking as much as two and three-quarter hours to go round. It was later in 1909 that 'A Cinematograph Film of the recent match at Weybridge between Taylor and Horne was shown at the Electric Theatre, Marble Arch, Oxford Street'. By July 1912 an interesting report on a series of Kinemacolor pictures of the play in the foursomes at Hoylake contains a couple of sentences which perhaps bear out what I have been saying about Braid and Duncan:

These pictures are admirable, but an intensely comic effect is given to them by the speed at which the players are represented playing. Even the slow and methodical Braid appears playing at a rate that would put the lightning Duncan completely in the shade, and when Duncan himself appears playing out of a bunker he has leapt into the hazard, played the ball out and disappeared almost as soon as one realises his presence.

At the end of Thursday's two rounds Braid was seven shots behind Taylor's splendid 147, and Vardon, who had had a miserable 82 in the first round, was twelve shots off the pace, and completely out of it. Two young professionals, Charles Johns and Tom Ball, were closest to Taylor – but Johns, an unknown, was not expected to last the pace; Tom Ball was by now a highly respected threat. Sandy Herd was only four behind, but he always seemed to have one bad round, like his 80 the following morning. Duncan, as Bernard Darwin put it, 'is inclined to go up like a rocket and come down like the proverbial stick'. He had a second-round 82. Taylor continued to play fine golf and his total of 295 was quite unassailable. Braid did make up one of the seven shots during the final day's play, and that allowed him to be joint runner-up with Tom Ball. Johns was a stroke further back. Taylor had just one 6 in the four rounds of the Championship proper. He once said of his Championships, 'They are enjoyable only if you win easily' – and this was almost as easy as his eight-shot victory in 1900.

For the Jubilee Open at St. Andrews in 1910, conditions were at long last altered so that

The Golf Exhibition at St. Andrews, 1910, in its marquee behind the wall at the 17th green.

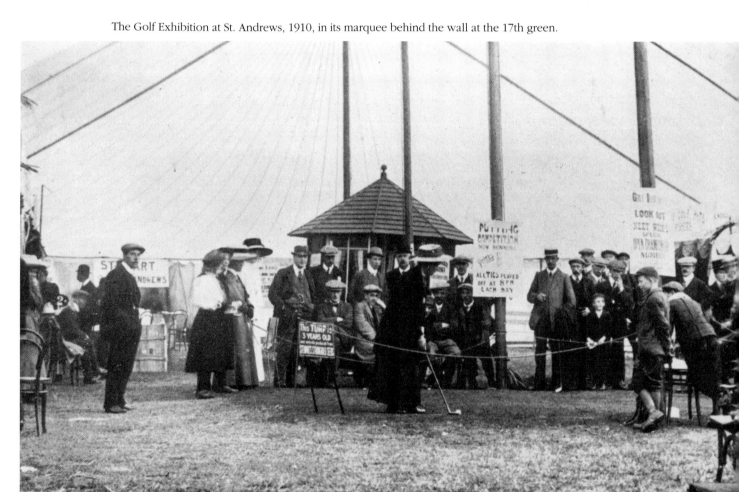

The Golfing Diploma issued at the time of the Jubilee Open in 1910 became a very popular Club prize.

only four rounds in all were to be played, unless the weather caused play to be suspended:

> The scores of the qualifying rounds shall count in the grand total, and the first sixty players and any who may tie among that number shall play two further rounds to decide the winner . . .

On the Tuesday, just after Braid had set out at 1.15, the weather broke. A storm of thunder and lightning lasted for about three-quarters of an hour, and the thunder-plump submerged several of the holes so that a putt sent the ball floating over the top. While the Championship Committee met hurriedly with a view to deciding what to do, out on the course many strange things were happening. One prominent golfer had six putts on the second green; some were using their niblicks to pitch into the holes; others were getting some holes marked on the card as 'unplayable'. Matters reached a crisis when one player who had approached over the Swilcan to the first green found the hole in the midst of a miniature lake. He indicated to those behind that he could not get near the hole, 'and holding that it was unplayable he determined to leave his ball at rest until a decision was arrived at'. This meant that for half an hour no one drove from the first tee. The Committee declared the day's play null and void, a decision perfectly covered by the then Rule 2, sub-section 2. When Braid was given the news, he had reached the 13th, and to make quite sure that there was no risk of disqualification if he had been misinformed, he completed the round in a fine 76, equalling Massy and Fernie who had finished before the weather broke down. But he had it all to do again the next day – and duly recorded a 76. Darwin had followed Harry Vardon whose 77, on paper, was a perfectly normal good round; but his description of Vardon's short putting is surely of 'the yips':

> When the ball is within three feet of the hole, Vardon's right wrist seems to become absolutely rigid and paralysed and instead of taking back the club well away from the ball he jerks it back about two inches with a stiff, nervous little movement. It was really a heart-breaking spectacle, because the rest of his game was absolutely perfect. In his 77 there were three short putts missed which may be fairly described as infantile.

It says much for Vardon's courage that, although like Taylor he would finish this time over a dozen strokes behind the winner, Braid, he would win two more Opens before the First World War began in August, 1914.

The best round of the first day was Duncan's 73; yet it could have been decidedly better. He was three below fours standing on the fourteenth tee; a bad push led to a six. At the sixteenth, a long drive finished on the railway line. He could only play it even further right to get clear and the result was again a six. He got a five all right at the Road hole, and then ran down a five-yard putt for a three at the last. A little ominously, this account ended with: 'Throughout he played with perfect confidence, and never wasted any time looking at his putts.'

The highlight of the second day's play was a record-equalling 71 from Willie Smith. Now a professional in Mexico, and American Open Champion in 1899, he had learnt to play golf in his native Carnoustie. As he was in the very last couple, coming in after 7.30 p.m., he upset all the pressmen's morning introductions, when he holed a five-yard putt on the final green. After 36 holes he led by one shot from Braid and two from Duncan.

For the final two rounds on the Friday, Duncan was first off at 7.35 a.m. with a wet grey haar hanging about and the greens covered in dew. Out in 36, he had played beautifully, but Darwin noted that 'he now seemed a little uncomfortable on the green and was moving his head and body forward as he struck the ball as if with an excess of anxiety to see where it was going'. But he was still holing the putts, and equalled Smith's 71, the highlights being quite beautiful fours at both the 14th and 17th. The ball would not drop for Braid on several long putts but hung obstinately on the lip, so that his one birdie was a steady four at the fourteenth. The 17th might well have ended Braid's chances. He slipped and topped his second, leaving himself that fiendishly difficult shot in from the left, about a hundred yards out. He pulled it slightly and got the Road bunker. The moment was critical: if he went on to the road from there, he could have taken anything. He played a great shot and nearly got a five. He was two behind Duncan at the end of the morning's play. Willie Smith had taken 80 with an eight at the 14th, and as an American visitor remarked, 'He was Willie Smith of Carnoustie yesterday after his 71 – now he's taken 80, he's just plain Smith the Yankee!'

Duncan's fourth round started at 12.35, and 'he showed signs of very palpable if natural anxiety . . . He was constantly weak and short in his approaching and early on got fours by the skin of his teeth by holing difficult putts . . . Sixes at both the 5th and 6th were disastrous and although he steadied for a while, from the 14th to the end one calamity succeeded another, and his golf may be fairly called demoralized.' It all added up to an 83. Darwin added prophetically, 'His time for winning the Championship is bound to come, for he is a beautiful golfer'. His time came a long ten years later in 1920. Herd with a 76 now crept in a shot ahead of Duncan, and but for finishing 6, 5, he would have been closer than four shots behind Braid. Once again Braid's steadiness pulled him through. Duncan undeniably was more brilliant at times; but on the Old Course stretched to its utmost and with the holes deliberately put close to bunkers, Braid showed that it is 'dogged that does it'. His final 76 left him a comfortable winner of the gold medal, the Jubilee Commemoration Medal, £50 and the right of holding the Golf Champion Trophy for a year. This was to be his fifth and last. By 1911 his eyes were giving him trouble, and he would no longer dominate the Open Championship as he had done for a full decade.

My abiding memory of him is towards the end of his life, perhaps in 1949, when from my position on the high ground near the third tee on Elie, I watched him cross from his native Earlsferry to the 18th tee, play a beautiful drive far up the fairway, and stride away, a tall, majestic figure, followed by an admiring crowd.

CHAPTER 14

END OF THE GOLDEN AGE:
WAR – AND PEACE: 1911 TO 1919

BETWEEN 1911 AND 1914 none of the Opens was contested on St. Andrews Links so that these need not detain us long.

Bernard Darwin always maintained that the 1911 Open at Sandwich was the most exciting ever. Very often, as we have seen, these Championships have resolved themselves into a duel or at most a three-cornered fight – unless as in Braid's and Taylor's case they sometimes won by a street. In 1911 it was a journalist's nightmare: at one time or another Duncan, Vardon and Hilton all had the chance of a lifetime, and flung it away, especially

St. Andrews caddies, 1870, 1900, 1930. St. Andrews University, Cowie Collection.

James Braid, Harry Vardon and Ted Ray, c. 1910. D. C. Thomson & Co Ltd., Dundee.

Vardon when he had a three-shot lead. It was left to Massy, that very tough competitor, to succeed in catching Vardon. In fact his last putt but one trembled on the lip or he would have won outright. The 36 hole play-off was almost anti-climax: Vardon's golf was nearly perfect; he led by five after eighteen holes, and by ten at the end of the thirty-fourth. Eventually Massy picked up his ball from a bad lie near the thirty-fifth green, extended his hand with a great grin, and said, 'I cannot play this damned game!'

1912 at Muirfield was Ted Ray's Open. A massive man, worth backing in any long-driving competition, he was as forthright as Andra Kirkaldy. He will always be remembered for his advice to a pupil wanting the secret of longer driving: 'Hit it a —— sight harder, mate!' In the 1912 Open he had to overcome the challenge of Vardon, Braid and Duncan, but it was hardly even that since in the end he was four ahead of Vardon, eight ahead of Braid and ten ahead of Duncan. A much greater challenge faced Ray's supporters as he left the last green. Several of them insisted on hoisting his colossal form on their shoulders, a task which very nearly proved too much for them.

At Hoylake in 1913 the qualifying rounds produced one surprise and very nearly another. Duncan was eliminated by several shots, his driving being erratic and his approaching and putting very faulty. Taylor qualified by the skin of his teeth, in a tie for last place. Yet Taylor became the 1913 Open Champion, drawing himself level at five Championships with Braid and Vardon. This was an early indication that the present method of exempting certain entrants and making all the others play two qualifying rounds is the best answer. On the final day in **1913 it had boiled down to a duel between Taylor and Ray, who seemed to have a huge advantage in length and strength. But in this case 'a strong blustery wind was blowing across at many holes'** – and Taylor's matchless straightness in a cross wind was the decisive factor. Once again, Darwin commented on Vardon's putting: 'Vardon as usual came well up on the list – if he could only putt he would never be anything else but at the very top of it . . .' One photograph, a sad one, showed Braid playing in tinted glasses, and he finished well down the field. It would have been nice to have a snap of the incident when Taylor was playing his final hole. He had to wait while 'a small black puppy was shouted at, was waved at with flags and cajoled by different officials. Taylor bore it nobly and stood like a graven image till the puppy disappeared. Then he tackled his delicate pitch over a bunker, went into rough over the green, pitched back beautifully and holed a three-footer.' No one else had a chance.

In June, 1914 at Prestwick, just a few weeks before 'the lamps were going out all over Europe,' there was what proved to be the final Open Championship battle between Vardon and Taylor. After the first 36 holes this was how Darwin summed up the situation:

> With all respect to the young ones, those two terrible old gentlemen, Vardon and Taylor, seem likely to fight it out to the end. They are drawn to play together, and Heaven help those who have to steward the match.' He went on to describe the final day: 'Never have they had to play before so terrific a crowd. For some six hours they fought their hand-to-hand fight in a ring enclosed by some six or seven thousand spectators, and two more exhausted men never tottered up to the home putting green than were these two at the end of it all. Vardon's aggregate score was 306, Taylor's 309.

The turning point had come at the fourth hole in the final round where Taylor, having had a disastrous 6 in the morning through being bunkered on the left, tried the other line and was bunkered on the right. He just got out, but his ball lay awkwardly and he pushed his next into the burn. He had to drop another, and put it over the green; three putts completed the tragedy, and he holed out in 7. Vardon had a steady 4 and from two behind was now one ahead. At the next, Taylor, showing every sign of strain, put his pitch well short and then, to the horror of his supporters, raced his putt about eight yards past: Vardon 4, Taylor 5. That hole, the Himalayas, completed the work that the fourth had begun. So Vardon stands as the only six times winner of the Championship.

Before the first postwar Open in 1920, won at last by George Duncan, there was a very important change in the running of the Championship. Until then both the Open and the Amateur had been organised and controlled by a consortium of 24, later 26, golf clubs, the actual conduct of each Championship being in the hands of the Club on whose course it was being held. When the consortium met on 8th December, 1919 it decided almost unanimously that the R&A become supreme authority for the management of the two championships and, for this purpose, appoint a committee of representative golfers with executive powers. Accordingly 'The Royal and Ancient Golf Club Championship Committee', to give it its full title, was formed.

CHAPTER 15

JOCK HUTCHISON
IN THE GROOVE, 1921

*T*O THIS POINT I HAVE SUPPLIED INFORMATION ABOUT CHAMPIONSHIPS other than at St. Andrews, because no one has covered them up to 1914 in any detail. From here on, our Opens have been far better documented, so that I propose to use material hitherto untapped such as reports in the *St. Andrews Citizen* and Bernard Darwin's accounts in *The Times* as available on microfilm in St. Andrews University Library.

For 1921, Mr Tom Rodger, then an apprentice architect, can lend one or two other eye-witness touches. He particularly noted the contrast between the Old School, Braid and Taylor, with their tweed trousers and jackets, and Walter Hagen, one of the new American stars, with his white shirt, black bow tie, black and white diced plus fours, black and white diamond-pattern stockings and black and white shoes. Hagen, who won our Open four times between 1922 and 1929, set the fashion in golfing dress throughout the 1920s. The 1921 reports seem to have omitted any reference to Jock Hutchison's 'ribbed' iron; but Mr Rodger noted his expert way of pitching past the hole and spinning sharply back towards it. The *Citizen*'s reporter expressed his disapproval a fortnight after Hutchison became Champion: '. . . we do not use the "ribbed" club, because it marks the ball so badly; and as we do not get our balls for nothing like the "crack" professionals, the expense of using the "ribbed" club would be out of all proportion to the benefits gained.' Before, during and at the prize-giving after the Championship, no such sentiments were expressed.

Jock Hutchison, born and bred in St. Andrews, had learnt his golf there and, just before the War, had emigrated, like so many other fine Scottish professionals, to the United States. Now an American citizen, he started as a favourite for the 1921 Open, a position he fully justified by heading the qualifiers and breaking the record for the Eden Course with a 69. Robert Tyre Jones Jnr. was then the leading amateur in this, his first British Open. It has often been said that he walked the course backwards – the original way of playing it – so as to see all the hidden bunkers, especially at the twelfth hole. Phil Harison, a member of Augusta National, played golf with Jones many times, and confirms that this was the case. But it cannot have been on his first visit. He was bunkered during a practice round, and someone said, 'You surely didn't know that bunker was there, Bobby'. The *Citizen* reported his reply as, 'Gee! I sure didn't'.

It was in the first round of the Championship proper that Jock Hutchison achieved his remarkable scores at the eighth and ninth holes. His playing partner was the immortal 'Bobby'. (He was my boyhood hero, and I cannot use any other word.) Tom Rodger and Bernard Darwin were in the gallery, and as the latter described it, Jock's tee-shot at the eighth

was a perfect pitch and the ball rolled gently into the hole. At the ninth, 270 yards long,

1921: Jock Hutchison chips to the 2nd green. In the background, the footbridge over the railway. Bobby Jones reckoned that if Hutchison had had the proverbial Scottish dourness instead of a ready wit, he would have won more championships.

> he hit a tremendous tee-shot. The ground is hard and the wind was helping, and the ball
> positively lipped the hole for another one and remained stone dead . . .

There is this legend about a spectator dashing to the pin, hauling it out, and perhaps preventing the ball from going in. Neither of these eye-witnesses saw anything of the sort, it was never mentioned in any contemporary account, as far as I know, and surely Carl Lewis would have been pushed to reach that pin in time? But, as Bobby wrote in his *Down the Fairway* (1927):

> Tommy Kerrigan (an American who finished third) was on the green when Jock drove,
> not expecting to reach it . . .

Perhaps that is how the legend started.

It was in the third round that Bobby Jones went out in 46 and was so badly bunkered at the 11th that he was alleged to have torn up his card and thus retired from the contest. He had been the leading amateur after two rounds, a stroke ahead of Roger Wethered, an undergraduate at Oxford, who from that point on played quite wonderful golf since he made up six shots on Jock Hutchison and fully earned a play-off. That is perhaps a better way of looking at his achievement than, say, suggesting that he would have won had he not trod on his ball at the fourteenth in the third round. In the final rounds Wethered had been allowed to start early because he could then catch a train and arrive in time to play in a cricket match elsewhere! There was less likelihood of amateur status being endangered in those days.

Going into the final round, Jim Barnes, the Cornishman turned American, was leading on 222, Wethered with a splendid 72, including that penalty shot, was on 225, two behind Arnaud Massy and the great Australian trickshot player, Joe Kirkwood. Hutchison had had a miserable time with his putter, took 79, and was on 226. He was playing not far behind Wethered in the final round so that, towards the end, he knew that even a 69 might be needed to force a play-off. For the amateur was on course, for a brilliant 70. He had had five 3s round the loop, driving the tenth and twelfth greens, and almost getting on the ninth as well. Darwin described his final hole:

> At the eighteenth he had a fine, long drive, level with Rusack's Hotel: had he known the ground in front of the green he would have known that there is a treacherous slow patch.

Even in the 1920s, arrangements for removing puddles from St. Andrews greens remained primitive.

He played what he thought was a good shot, and it turned out dreadfully short. Almost inevitably he took three more from the Valley of Sin.

Jock Hutchison then needed a four to tie, and very nearly managed a three, his second shot being no more than five yards from the pin.

The play-off emphasised the difference between a great amateur player and a hardened professional with vast experience gained all over the world. Eventually Jock won by nine shots over the 36 holes, Roger Wethered struggling to an 82 in the second round.

At the presentation afterwards, it was very unfortunate that the Chairman of the Green Committee was thoroughly boorish in handing over the Golf Champion Trophy. A letter in the *Citizen* said, 'Mr Wethered played like a sportsman and heartily congratulated the winner; but the Chairman of the Green Committee was such a poor loser that he practically threw the cup at Hutchison, did not call for cheers for the new Champion – instead he at once called for "Three cheers for Roger Wethered".' This unfortunate incident was to some extent balanced by a gracious speech from John Henry Taylor: 'It is perfectly true that "Jock" Hutchison has come here under the thin disguise of an American, but, looking under the veneer, we see a style redolent of the great Scottish champions of the past.' Now, for the first time in Open Championship history, the Trophy would cross the Atlantic.

'J.H.' was not quite so complimentary a little later when he joined in speaking out against the 'ribbed' club used by Hutchison – and one or two others – as 'buying the shot out of the shop'. A month before the 1921 Open began, there was a very interesting minute when the Rules of Golf Committee met at Hoylake on 25th May:

Corrugated Clubs

After full consideration it was decided that grooved and slotted Iron Clubs (or any clubs which have the surface of the face fashioned in any manner in order to produce the same effect) do not conform to the conditions set out in the clause on 'Form and Make of Golf Clubs' and that the use of them after 1st July, 1921 shall be considered illegal.

'It was further decided that nothing in the foregoing resolution is to be regarded as barring the use of clubs lightly scored or punched in the manner which has long been customary.'

The notice about it was published in the *Citizen* of 2nd July, 1921, right alongside the final scores in the Championship.

It was at Tom Rodger's suggestion that many years later, Jock Hutchison was approached and readily agreed to present his 'ribbed' club to the Royal & Ancient Golf Club.

CHAPTER 16

BOBBY'S SECOND OPEN: ST. ANDREWS, 1927

*T*HE YEAR 1926 IS FOREVER LINKED with an extraordinary event in British history, the General Strike. But in that year, Bobby Jones would also win his first Open Championship, at Lytham, Lancashire. In 1921 he had retired at the eleventh hole of his third round at St. Andrews, but, as he explained later, he had not actually torn up his card. He completed the round and then had a fine 72 in the afternoon. He was now 24, the U.S. Amateur Champion for the past two years; but more significantly he had won the U.S. Open in 1923, and would win it again in 1926, 1929 and 1930.

The highlight of the Lytham Open in 1926 was undoubtedly Bobby's remarkable shot of at least 160 yards from a bunker at the seventeenth in the final round. The draw for the last 36 holes had paired him with Al Watrous who at one point in the final round was the Championship leader by two shots; but they were level standing on the 17th tee. Bobby then hooked into a

Bobby Jones with J. H. Taylor at Lytham and St. Anne's, 1926. This was Jones' first Open victory in Britain, but Taylor, aged 56, shot a 71 in a gale in the third round, better than any round of Bobby's.

J. H. Taylor in 1931. Born 1870, still going strong. *Dundee Courier.*

Bobby Jones: a study in concentration.

shallow bunker, and when Watrous had found the green with his second he must have felt he was in command. He was visibly shaken when Bobby with his mashie-iron, about a 4 iron, took the ball beautifully cleanly and finished on the green 'inside' Watrous' ball. Almost inevitably Watrous then three-putted and Bobby went on to win by a single stroke. There is a plaque in that bunker to this day, commemorating what was really the winning shot; and the mashie-iron is in the Royal Lytham and St. Anne's Clubhouse.

John Henry Taylor like his fellow-members of the Triumvirate was now nearer 60 than 50, but coming in a remarkable eleventh equal he actually had a 71, better than any single round of Bobby's!

At St. Andrews in 1927 bookmakers created a sensation during the qualifying rounds by taking up their stance beside the starter's box and shouting the odds of '10 to 1 Jones, 30 to 1 Barnes' and so on. But Jimmy Alexander, the starter, very soon moved them on.

For the first time, white lines had been painted round the greens to indicate that spectators 'must not enter the circle', and this scheme worked remarkably well.

With a cut-off at 160 after the qualifying rounds, the old Champions did well: Braid (150), Taylor (155), Vardon and Herd (156). Not for the first time, George Duncan the 1920 Champion, thirteen to fifteen years their junior, failed to qualify. Cheape's bunker destroyed him during his second round. This underlines what Bobby said soon after he had won:

> There was always something in the way, some dreaded place on every hole which I felt I must avoid. The grand old course still needs a lot of playing and no one realises this better than I do.

In the first round of the Championship proper, Bobby had a quite remarkable 68, remarkable because of the number of putts he sank, ranging from forty yards at the long fifth to three of ten yards, and various others rather shorter. Darwin pointed out that he was seldom near with his approaches – but he holed everything after that. Like Braid in his prime, Bobby could be putting for a three at the fifth when lesser players were struggling, with a blind shot over the hollow from about wedge distance. There was one rather poignant moment when Harry Vardon, once the centre of attraction, was standing unnoticed protecting his ball while the crowd crushed past in their anxiety to miss nothing that Bobby was doing.

1927: the final round. The crowd negotiates the Swilcan.

In 1936 Bobby Jones returned to St. Andrews to play before admiring crowds.

That 68 put him three clear strokes ahead of the field, but in effect it did more than that. Apart from Joe Kirkwood with a 72 there was no one within six shots of him who was likely to last the course. Havers, the 1923 Champion, had a sad 80; he was level with Bobby over the next three rounds and did very well to come seventh equal along with a very young Henry Cotton. Apart from the actual winner, the players who added most to their reputations were Aubrey Boomer, like Vardon and Ray a Channel Islander, and Fred Robson, who tied for second place with 291, a score which in any previous year would have at least forced a play-

off for the Championship. Both had been eight shots back after one round, so that making up two strokes after that on Bobby's 285 was highly creditable. Bobby had had to struggle here and there: he was bunkered from his drive at the second in every round but the third; he had holed that virtually impossible putt, a thirty-yarder from the top left-hand corner of the eleventh green. In the final round he had a huge drive at the seventh very near to Shell bunker: 'a camera fiend clicked his fiendish instrument and the great man fluffed his pitch into the bunker almost in front of his nose.' The result was a five. But he had four consecutive threes after that, 'and the door was firmly closed against the rest'.

There were many other good rounds as Bernard Darwin put it, 'but the Championship was over when Bobby Jones was over'. He went on:

Another moment from the 1936 visit. Bobby Jones with Willie Auchterlonie to his right and ex-Provost Boase of St. Andrews to his left.

As soon as the last putt was holed the greater part of the multitude (about 15,000 in the area) surged up the slope . . . and enveloped the champion. Even Captain Lindbergh in Paris or at Croydon cannot have been in more imminent fear of asphyxiation than was the champion for one or two anxious moments. Then clasping his famous "Calamity Jane" tightly in his hand he was hoisted upon willing shoulders while hundreds of hands patted him on the back or any other available portion of him. The crowd swung this way and that with its burden. Bobby's cap was soon irretrievably lost, but still he held his putter inviolate over his head. At long last he was safely on the ground again, and the admiring crowd followed him, gazing and patting until he was safe in his hotel.

In 1927, he and Walter Hagen were the only players to have won the Open Championships on both sides of the Atlantic more than once; and Bobby was of course the only amateur who had held both titles even once. He and Harold Hilton were the only amateurs who had won our Open Championship twice, and Bobby the only one to win it twice in succession, a feat no one had achieved since James Braid won in 1905 and 1906. No one at this time would have thought for a moment that in 1930 Bobby would achieve the Grand Slam, the Open and

The cannon used when the Captain plays himself in. *Dundee Courier.*

In 1935, while still Provost, W. Norman Boase played himself in as new Captain of the Royal and Ancient Golf Club to the customary ceremonial gunfire. *Dundee Courier.*

Amateur Championships of both Britain and the United States – and then retire at the very zenith of his golfing career.

What a contrast there was between Jock Hutchison's reception when the trophy was presented in 1921, and Bobby's in 1927. In those days professionals were frequently denied access to clubhouses, and Walter Hagen would in these circumstances arrive in a Rolls Royce, and change his shoes in the car! Now the greatest amateur of them all had won and, although this was the sixth American victory in seven years, the Cup would for once not cross the Atlantic. Bobby, an honorary member of the Royal & Ancient, announced at the presentation that he would like to leave it in the custody of the Club. He was, as I have said, my boyhood hero; but it was only many years later that I came to realise quite what a splendid choice I had made.

CHAPTER 17

TRIUMPH AND DISASTER:
1933

THE AMERICAN PROFESSIONALS WERE HERE IN FULL STRENGTH for the Ryder Cup in 1933; and, when it was contested at Southport a few weeks before our Open Championship, Great Britain won by the narrowest margin, a single putt on the last green. Syd Easterbrook was the British hero, beating Denny Shute in that final match when the American three-putted. But in our Open it was Shute who triumphed, and one disaster or another befell not only his British opponents but several American ones as well.

My abiding memory of St. Andrews during the 1933 Open was of parched brown fairways where the ball seemed to roll on forever. Modern fertilisers and weed-killers – so necessary when the traffic on the Old Course is almost unending between April and November – have totally changed the character of the turf. It can be just as burnt up; but only Fred Couples (during the practice rounds for the 1984 Open) succeeded in reaching and in fact bouncing over the Swilcan Burn at the first hole. During the final round in 1933, several found themselves in the Burn, and soon most players were taking an iron from the first tee. Small wonder when, as a thirteen-year-old, I could then drive the first green on the Eden Course, a distance of 265 yards.

The stewarding arrangements in 1933 were very good, even if one instruction read rather ominously, 'Shouting and swearing must not be indulged in by officials'.

In the 1933 qualifying rounds, Craig Wood showed just what a lack of local knowledge can mean to you when he took 82 round the Old Course. In the end he qualified with four shots to spare; and he had learnt so much by the third round of the Championship proper that he achieved a 68, on his way to tying with Denny Shute for the Championship.

On the Wednesday, during the first round of the Open, there were several interesting and even exciting episodes. Hagen with a fine 68 led the field. Sandy Herd, now 65, and playing with the holder, Gene Sarazen, fell over in making a shot out of the rough at the tenth and hurt his ankle so badly that he could hardly go on. He had qualified a shot ahead of both Shute and Wood! It was that day that another spectator nudged me and whispered 'Vardon!' I was standing beside the great man. Later I was following Archie Compston and Henry Cotton, and at the thirteenth Compston was five below fours, Cotton level. At this point the Prince of Wales, a member of Compston's Club, Coombe Hill, arrived on the scene – and for Compston the magic soon vanished. He began to show off, asking a small boy what club he should take for a comparatively short second at the fifteenth, and fluffing into a bunker. Eventually he took 72 and was obviously furious as he left the last green. Cotton was only a shot behind him, an indication of how professional his approach was. On the Wednesday night there was a very pleasant interlude when all the American players visited the Cathedral grounds, and Walter

The Prince of Wales and Archie
Compston, 1933.

Leo Diegel. Those who copied him were
'Diegeling'.

Hagen laid a wreath at the graves of Old and Young Tom Morris.

On the Thursday Hagen held his lead with a 72, and Abe Mitchell – reckoned very unlucky never to have won the Open – had a fine 68. There has always been some confusion about Sarazen's misfortunes while defending the title he had won at Princes, Sandwich, in 1932. Did he go three over par by getting into Hill bunker on the left of the eleventh green described by Darwin as 'the most dreadful bunker in all golf? Or did he have an 8 at the fourteenth having visited the dreaded Hell? The answer is both. In the second round he took three to get clear of Hill. The little American's head was scarcely visible as he was seen to swing the club once, twice, three times before he reached the green. Many thought that he had taken four to get out, a rumour which persisted until the evening when the Championship Committee confirmed that he had taken 6, not 7. Leo Diegel, he of the strange putting style, should have matched Mitchell's 68, but he drifted into the Road Bunker at the seventeenth,

took two to get out, and was lucky to get a 6. For once there were few real disasters at that hole; the fifth once, and the fourteenth twice, affected the outcome considerably during the final round.

After the third round, on the Friday morning, the scoreboard showed that Syd Easterbrook, Abe Mitchell and Henry Cotton were joint leaders with Leo Diegel and the Australian, Joe Kirkwood. Craig Wood's fine 68 had brought him right back into the reckoning; but Walter Hagen's 79 was disastrous. He was never interested in being second, and in fact finished with an 82. Meanwhile Densmore Shute produced his third 73, almost unwatched by any gallery; he was three off the pace, and quite unconsidered. Sarazen, a shot better at this point, was highly fancied.

Nowadays when the scores of the leading players are promptly posted at various vantage points for all to read, it is difficult to visualise the situation in 1933. There was one large scoreboard on the Bow Butts behind the R&A Clubhouse, just beyond the bandstand – and that was all. The 'talkies' had replaced silent films several years before this; but the 'walkie-talkie' arrived much later. The first reference to it that I can find is a pencilled note on the back of a 1946 Open Programme. At lunchtime after the third round a winning total of 284 or 285 was freely spoken of; Sarazen in conservative mood said 287; in the end Shute and Wood tied at 292.

In that final round, players with a good chance of winning cracked and threw it away. Craig Wood was, of course, terribly unlucky to find the left-hand bunker on the ridge in front of the fifth green, a drive of about 430 yards. The hole cost him a five, and perhaps an

Fans

The start of Craig Wood's quite unnecessary six.

outright victory in the Championship. But he had a quite unnecessary six at the fifteenth. Kirkwood broke up badly. Cotton had a brace of sixes running in his 79. Mitchell wrecked himself by pitching his first mashie shot into the burn and taking 39 out. Easterbrook, wanting only three fives and two fours to win, with the wind lulling in his favour had a seven at the fourteenth. Sarazen stood on the fourteenth tee in the really threatening position of two under fours. But his visit to Hell Bunker cost him an eight. 'I never dreamt,' said Sarazen afterwards, 'that they would all crash and that 292 would have a chance.' If he had had any doubt he could have played safely out of Hell instead of going for the green and remaining in it. The most extraordinary lapse of all came from Leo Diegel, who was doing so well that Darwin 'backed the wrong horse' and followed him for the last five holes. At the final hole, Diegel had two putts to tie with Shute and Wood, but as Darwin put it: 'Finally he laid his putt apparently stone-dead in three at the Home Hole and missed the putt by the widest possible margin' – a very kindly way of describing an air-shot!

The play-off was really an anti-climax after all that. Shute started with two 4s, Wood with two 6s, and from then on the writing was on the wall. A 74 and a 75 were good enough to bring Shute victory by five shots. He had not broken par in any one of his six rounds, but he had played more steadily than anyone else.

This was perhaps the nadir for British Open golf; Arthur Havers had been our last Champion,

102

Right
Willie Park Senior, first Open Champion, at
Prestwick in 1860, by John A.T. Bonnar about 1887

Old Tom Morris, at 81, by Sir George Reid

Andrew Kirkaldy, Hon. Professional to the R & A, 1910-34

Willie Auchterlonie, Open Champion 1893

Right

'The Triumvirate', by Clement Flower, 1913. John Henry Taylor, James Braid and Harry Vardon won the Open trophy sixteen times between them from 1894 to 1914

Vardon, Braid and Taylor, from a tinted postcard of about 1910

Signs of the times: 'and Ladies' Golf' was added to 'Golfing' a week after World War I began; by September this advertisement had appeared

Bobby Jones by J.A.A. Berrie. This portrait hangs at the Royal Liverpool Golf Club, Hoylake

Gene Sarazen, a study by Abel Petit, the famous
French cartoonist

GENE SARAZEN

the sturdy American who finished
second to Hagen in the Open
Championship.
A study by Abel Petit, the famous
French Cartoonist.

Henry Cotton by J.A.A. Berrie.
'Redeemer of British Golf', he won the
Open in 1934, 1937 and 1948

The modern scene: stands around the first and eighteenth holes, St Andrews, 1984

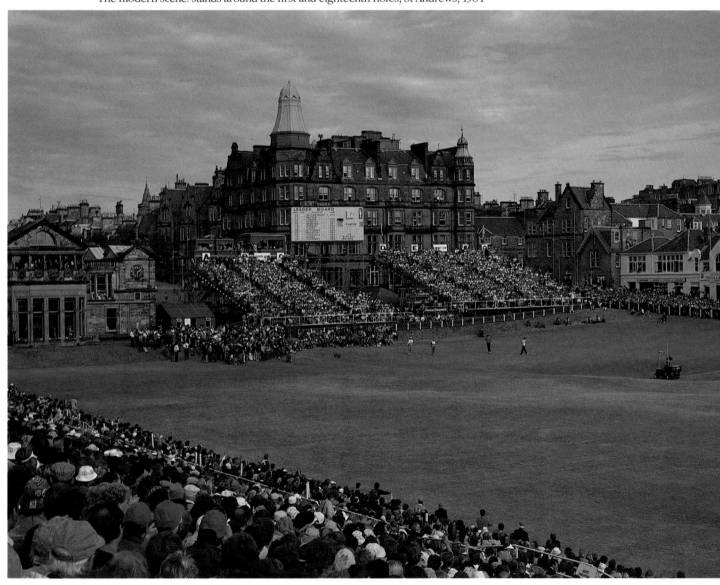

The 1984 Open: contestants finishing out at the eighteenth, with the Royal and Ancient Clubhouse as backdrop

Opposite top
The famous – or notorious – Valley of Sin. Behind is the Starter's Box. Another scene from the 1984 Open

Opposite lower
The seventeenth, or Road Hole

Jack Nicklaus, Open Champion – again – in 1978

Opposite
1984: Baker-Finch's battling four at the seventeenth

Opposite top
Lee Trevino, between bouts of filming 'The Trevino Connection' at St Andrews

Opposite lower
Nick Faldo, by far the most consistent British competitor in the British Open since 1978

1984, and the final round. It's between Tom Watson and Seve Ballesteros, but Watson's second shot has put him two feet from the wall at the seventeenth. Ballesteros is on the eighteenth

The moment of triumph. The final putt has gone down, and Seve Ballesteros is 1984 Open Champion

Ballesteros driving at the seventeenth on his way to victory in the 1984 Open

. . . and peace returns to the Old Course at St Andrews

Walter Hagen in 1933, by now a senior player, on his way to a 79. St. Andrews University, Cowie
Collection.

Gene Sarazen at the sixteenth, soon after
that dreadful 8.

Densmore Shute, Champion 1933, at his
first appearance.

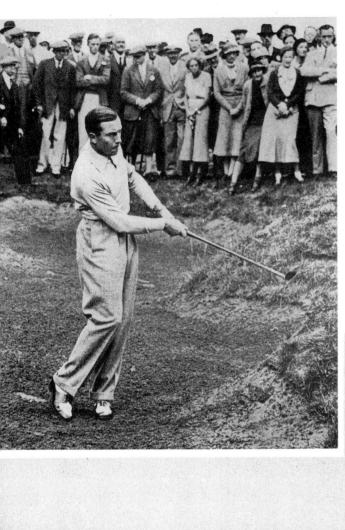

Henry Cotton, redeemer of British Golf.
Open Champion 1934, 1937, 1948.
Evening Telegraph, Dundee.

in 1923. Between 1934 and 1939 all the winners were in fact British; but the finest American players were no longer coming over, probably because money was tight, except in 1937 for the Ryder Cup. When Cotton won the Open at Carnoustie that year it was against the entire American team, the zenith of his and British golf, and with victories also in 1934 and 1948 he was our greatest champion since the days of the Triumvirate. Post-war, Daly (1947) and Faulkner (1951) were also winners, but the next great peak would be 1969/70 when Jacklin held both the Open Championships, British and American, simultaneously.

CHAPTER 18

DICK BURTON STOPS THE ROT: 1939

WHEN DICK BURTON BECAME THE 1939 CHAMPION he broke the run of American victories which had haunted St. Andrews since Jock Hutchison's win in 1921. True, the American challenge was not nearly as strong as it had been in 1927 or 1933: there was a comparative unknown, Johnny Bulla, who as a non-member of the American PGA was ineligible for the Ryder Cup; and Lawson Little, the great Amateur champion of 1934 and 1935, now a professional. The favourites were Cotton; A.D. 'Bobby' Locke, still in his 'teens but a marvellous player whose turn would come four times, post-war; and Jimmy Bruen,

A slim young Bobby Locke at St. Andrews, July 1939. Note the wet-weather clothing to combat nasty conditions.

the nineteen-year-old Irish boy whose looped swing and tremendous power allied to a beautiful short game astonished the crowds. In 1939 an average of 5,000 people paid per day, and nearly all went with only three matches – Cotton, Locke and Bruen.

Less than a year before, in September, 1938, war had seemed inevitable, and no one, especially aged seventeen and upwards at that time, will ever forget the black despair which gripped the nation. The industrial depression throughout the 1930s had been terrible enough. Millions were literally 'on the breadline'; poverty was not then linked with the loss of beer, cigarettes and television. In Glasgow's streets you could see children with rickets, bent limbs brought on by malnutrition; and ex-servicemen with trays of matches were more or less begging for pennies. In Munich that September, Neville Chamberlain had acquired 'a piece of paper' signed by Hitler and himself which he declared meant 'peace in our time'. The relief was tremendous; but from early 1939 the threat of war kept growing. By July 1939 and the Open Championship, only a minority can have felt that the uneasy peace would last for very long.

For the 1939 Championship a number of important changes had been made to the Old Course: in particular, new 'tiger' tees had been built at the 5th and the 14th, stretching these holes to 576 and 564 yards respectively. It was explained that 'these tees are situated further from the lines along which spectators congregate, to simplify crowd control and give the players more room when playing from these tees'. As we shall see, the new tee at the 14th created great problems for several fancied competitors. Among these would have been Alf Padgham, the 1936 Champion, but he had forgotten to enter, just as in the previous year Percy Alliss had been guilty of a similar oversight.

As so frequently happens, the qualifying rounds were led by players none of whom finished in the first eight of the Championship proper. The most startling failure was that of Lawson Little who followed up his 69 and 73 in the qualifying stage with 79 and 80 and was not within eight strokes of securing a place for the last 36 holes on the Friday. Bruen, who had had two fine 69s to lead the qualifiers, six under fours, was ten over in the Championship proper. As Browning pointed out, the players who turn in these marvellous scores in qualifying deserve not congratulations but commiseration for being so unlucky as to hit their top form too soon.

An astonishing number of seasoned competitors could not believe that, with the wind against, the new tee at the 14th made it impossible to carry the 'Beardies' with their drive and 'Hell' with their second. The major casualty in the first round was Bobby Locke. He was six under fours standing on the fourteenth tee, having played quite flawless golf. He was caught in the 'Beardies', tried to make too much ground out of the bunker and left it still in. He barely got out with his third, tried the immensely long carry over 'Hell' and failed. In the end he sank a difficult putt for his eight. He finished with four brave fours. Has anyone else ever been round the Old Course in 70 with an eight? Locke tried to place his drive between the 'Beardies' and the boundary wall the next time, went out of bounds and had a seven. After that, not unnaturally, his golf deteriorated. It all amazed South Africans back home because, in four years of Championship golf, he had never been known to take as much as a six.

Dick Burton of Sale, a fair-haired Lancashire giant, had learnt the rudiments of the game knocking cotton reels about the waste ground of his native Darwen with a walking stick, and was now generally regarded as just about the longest driver in British professional golf.

Although he had a few wild drives, his immense power let him reach the green from places that would be quite impossible for most of his fellow professionals. In 1939 he had not peaked too soon – indeed, he qualified with only two shots to spare; but after the first two rounds proper he was in the lead. Johnny Bulla had opened with a 77, mainly because his putting was dreadful, and in practice he had used about six different putters. His usual centre-shafted one was unavailable, because, as a splendid cartoon illustrated, this type had been outlawed in Britain from 1910, and remained so until January, 1952. Henry Cotton started with a colourless 74, but was five under fours on the fourteenth tee in the second round. A visit to the 'Beardies' cost him a six, and, even more disastrous, an overhit second at the seventeenth landed on the Road and was over the wall in one ecstatic bounce: a seven and a round of 72 left him four behind Burton, three behind Martin Pose, a very fine Argentinian player, and two behind Johnny Fallon, a slight young Scot, who in the strong winds of the final round did not have the necessary power to cope, and had a 79. Cotton would now have two 76s and drop right out of the reckoning.

The main feature of the third round was a tragic eight at the seventeenth for the Argentinian, Martin Pose, because his caddie could not get him to understand that down by the wall he was in a hazard, the grass was part of it, and so he incurred a two-shot penalty by grounding his club. He had been very much in contention, but this incident threw him right out of his stride.

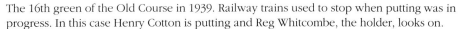

The 16th green of the Old Course in 1939. Railway trains used to stop when putting was in progress. In this case Henry Cotton is putting and Reg Whitcombe, the holder, looks on.

Johnny Bulla in his final round emerging from the railway yard; but he was playing the second and not the seventeenth at the time, and had pulled his drive a massive way left.

One journalist asked, 'Is it out of the question to provide foreign competitors with the local rules in their own language?' A Spanish translation was actually provided in 1946 – too late for Martin Pose. But for the penalty strokes he would have finished third. In that third round Burton's putting had been woeful and he slumped to a 77. Johnny Fallon led, and Johnny Bulla with two successive 71s was lying fourth alongside Burton and Pose.

In the final round, Bulla was an early starter, so early that he was playing the sixteenth as Burton went up the second. The two galleries were in contact and Burton soon knew that Bulla needed 4, 5, 4 for a 73 and a total of 292. He needed a 72 to beat Bulla, his main threat. Burton was playing very steadily, and by the loop he knew that he needed the equivalent of five threes to keep on target. Three of them he got, but the real crunch came at the eleventh, with that incredibly difficult putt from the back of the downsloping green, and Strath bunker waiting to receive his ball if he missed. It gathered speed, struck the back of the hole with a rattle, jumped in the air and dropped in for a birdie two. That was the lucky break he needed. Like Massy in 1907, he knew exactly what he had to do, and like him, he won by two shots. His eighteenth hole was really spectacular: a drive well over 300 yards brought him halfway between the road and the green; a splendid pitch put him five yards from the pin, and to his great credit he hit his putt firmly into the hole. That gave him a 71 in what were very testing conditions.

Dick Burton, Open Champion 1939. *Dundee Courier.*

Of course, Burton has always been regarded as a most unlucky champion; but he was thoroughly philosophical about it. Soon after this he joined the Royal Air Force, and when, years later, he was asked if he considered himself unlucky, he exclaimed, 'Unlucky? – I came through the war, didn't I, and that's a lot more than many did who were at St. Andrews that day'.

CHAPTER 19

THE FIRST POST-WAR OPEN: SAM SNEAD, ST. ANDREWS, 1946

B Y JULY 1946, the defensive blocks and anti-tank monoliths strewed along the West Sands, and the poles set up against the landing of enemy aircraft, had been removed. The four St. Andrews courses were in fine condition. But there were many seemingly insuperable obstacles in the way of those trying to stage an Open Championship. Some years ago I was lucky enough to find a file of 1946 correspondence in a shed by the Jubilee course, and some of the difficulties facing Paymaster Commander J.A. Storer Carson RNVR, Secretary of the R&A from 28th April onwards, and his Assistant Secretary, Hilda Kirkwood, are revealed there. I will take them in chronological order.

In April 1946, *Golf Monthly* apologised because paper restrictions left them no room for advertising the Championship, and added that they could not possibly produce the *Golfer's Handbook* before 1947. The paper shortage was a nightmare for Hilda Kirkwood. Commander Roe of the PGA wrote to say that she could send him a few entry forms but it would be several weeks before he could notify all his members. (He added that the 1907 Champion, Arnaud Massy, required clothing coupons to enable him to purchase clothes, and that he had taken up the matter with the Board of Trade.) In June the Dunlop Rubber Co. wrote to Commander Carson to say that they were sending twenty-four dozen Dunlop '65' golf balls for the use of Amateurs competing in the Open. They should be allowed two balls each for the first and second qualifying rounds. In late June, Carson was informed by a member of the Championship Committee that he had applied to the City bakeries for assistance with the catering for the Open: 'The present rationing is very severe. The most I can get from them is 12 Swiss Rolls at a cost of 1/6d each; out of this 144 cakes could be cut . . . Pies are out of the question on account of the restricted supplies of fat and meat.'

There had been one very useful wartime development. The successful use of portable wireless ('Walkie-Talkie') in small raids and later in battle meant that in 1946 it could be used for crowd control by providing the Chief Steward with information from strategic points on the course, and to give the Press up-to-the-minute scores. The maximum range of these Walkie-Talkies, four in number, was about a mile. In addition, scoreboards were manned at the 5th, 9th and 17th. As for the previous three Opens, the main scoreboard was alongside the bandstand behind the Clubhouse. These arrangements made it easier to introduce an entirely new method of crowd control. The Old and New courses were to be fenced off and spectators were expected to remain behind the fences, except for one or two recognised crossing places, so

The happy post-War spirit is evident as Roger Wethered, Captain of the R&A in 1946, strides down
the first fairway with General Eisenhower. St. Andrews University, Cowie Collection.

that the players would suffer few interruptions during the Championship.

The Open would not be televised before 1957, but there was a good deal of other media
interest in 1946. Surprisingly little coverage was provided by the BBC: 'From Monday to Friday
between 10 and 15 minutes past one; on Monday and Tuesday on the Scottish Home Service
between 6.55 and 7.00 in the evening; on Wednesday, Thursday and Friday, between 7.00 and
7.15 p.m. on the first two days and 7.00 and 7.30 p.m. on the last day.' But applications for
permits to film the Open were lodged by New York Times Photos, Universal News, Metro-
Goldwyn-Mayer Pictures Limited, and British Movietonews Limited. At the tenth tee in the
third round a cine-camera operator from one of these organisations upset Locke so much that
Leonard Crawley estimated that it cost the South African Champion four shots in the next five
holes.

The 1946 scoreboard beside the bandstand and behind the R&A Clubhouse. *Evening Telegraph,* Dundee.

In November 1945, *Golf Monthly* asked, 'Who will stop Byron Nelson?' and added 'Little Ben Hogan, reckoned as great as Nelson, is now demobilised and he will be here'. In the event, neither of them came over, but a strong American trio did arrive: Samuel Jackson Snead, Johnny Bulla and Lawson Little. Bobby Locke was coming: a letter from South Africa said, 'He is slower than ever!, but can do a 66 on a 75 scratch course'.

The holder, Dick Burton, stated in the letter accompanying his entry money, 'I shall bring the "Cup" with me'. The other main British challengers were Cotton, Dai Rees, the marvellous little Welshman, who would never quite win the Open, and Fred Daly who succeeded in 1947.

There was such a gale blowing when Snead intended to fly here that no plane could take off and eventually he reached St. Andrews for breakfast on the Friday morning before the Championship started. He had two days to learn the Old Course, no time to rest from his journey, and no practice at all on the New Course. On that Friday he hit hundreds of balls

Johnny Bulla, second in 1939, came second again in 1946. St. Andrews University, Cowie Collection.

'Slammin', Sam Snead plays an approach shot to the 1st green. St. Andrews University, Cowie Collection.

Sam Snead, Open Champion 1946 at his first appearance. His long hitting – he reached the 14th green in 2 each time – proved decisive.

using all his clubs, followed by 36 holes on the Old Course. Then he did admit he was slightly tired. He played well on the Saturday morning, but the weather was so atrocious in the afternoon that not even he ventured out. As Snead lay in bed resting, golfing gossip made Locke or Cotton the winner next week. But Snead's tremendous length was to prove a decisive factor. In the Championship proper he drove the tenth green three times out of four, with no wind assistance, and was on the 12th green twice; but it was his playing of the fourteenth that was especially impressive. It has always been generally regarded as among the very best par 5 holes; Snead played it as a four throughout, and got away with it.

On the first two days of the Championship there was some really brilliant play; Cotton had two great 70s; Locke's 74 and 69 were very fine; but the highlight was Rees' 67, equalling Bill Nolan's record set up in 1933. Bulla and Snead were not far away, but Lawson Little's play was very disappointing. The final day was blessed by good weather and the wind blew more or less consistently. But the course was playing several shots harder than in the early rounds, especially in the first nine holes. At lunchtime all the leaders remained in the running, a tightly packed bunch. Snead, Bulla and Rees were on 215; Cotton on 216; and Locke on 218. But apart from Locke who was out in 36 in the afternoon, the remainder destroyed their chances in the first few holes, and even Snead took 40 to the turn. Cotton had far too many fives. Dai Rees was at the top of his swing on the first tee when some well-meaning idiot shouted 'Good Old Wales!' and he opened with a horrible slice which resulted in a seven. Bulla too went off shakily. Locke was one under fours before three-putting the thirteenth, and still looked uncatchable – but of all things his putting continued to let him down, and with only one four in the last five holes he slumped to a 76. Bulla's six at the seventeenth led him to tie with Locke on 294. A very tired Cotton was one shot back with a 79, and poor Rees joined him with an 80. The door was wide open for Snead, remembering that his performance on the back nine had been uniformly fine throughout. He came home in 35 for a 75, and victory by four clear shots.

When Lord Wardington called on Snead to receive the trophy he was still in his bath; but soon he arrived and the very warm applause showed that the crowd knew that the right man had won. At the prizegiving Henry Cotton said perhaps jocularly, 'On behalf of the underfed British competitors who just did not have the stomach to finish the course, I hope we will be able to win back the Cup when we get some good steaks'.

CHAPTER 20

THOMSON'S SECOND WIN: ST. ANDREWS, 1955

B *ETWEEN 1949 AND 1958*, our Open was dominated by Bobby Locke and Peter Thomson apart from Max Faulkner's win at Royal Portrush in 1951 and Ben Hogan's at Carnoustie in 1953. Like Vardon and Braid, Locke had won three Opens in four years: 1949, 1950 and 1952; Thomson achieved three consecutive victories between 1954 and 1956, the first hat-trick since Bob Ferguson's in 1882. They made it four each, in 1957 and 1958 respectively; and Thomson joined the august company of Taylor and Braid when he won for the fifth time in 1965.

At St. Andrews in 1955 there were some strong contenders for Thomson's crown gained at Royal Birkdale in 1954. There was Locke, of course, and a very interesting American, Ed Furgol, winner of the U.S. Open in 1954, whose withered arm seemed somehow to add to his attraction. A tall, spare man with Cherokee blood in him, his physical disability did not prevent him from, for instance, driving the twelfth green. Byron Nelson was here, but now only a

Ed Furgol in trouble at the seventeenth. The fourteenth cost him two sevens in the Championship proper.

Peter Alliss in his pre-commentating days. *Dundee Courier.*

Max Faulkner, Charlie Ward, Ken Bousfield and Dai Rees. St. Andrews University, Cowie Collection.

shadow of his former greatness. Eric Brown, Cerda of the Argentine, O'Connor, Bousfield and Van Donck of Belgium would all be to the fore; but two over-40s, John Fallon and Frank Jowle, were to mount the closest challenge to Peter Thomson.

Jowle produced quite a sensation in the qualifying rounds when he had the temerity to hole the New Course in 63 strokes. This produced a fine headline 'Cheek by Jowle!'

For the first round as for most of the Championship the perfect weather conditions kept the scores very much together. Cotton and Thomson, champions with twenty years between them, were paired top of the bill. Cotton's 70 was excellent, while Thomson's 71 resulted from flawless play up to the green. It was a characteristic run by the holder, containing no long putts, just a series of very near misses which left him apparently unruffled. Locke's 74 resulted from 5s at the ninth and tenth, both normally birdie chances. The lean willowy amateur of pre-

John Fallon on his way to an outward 31 in the final round.

War years was now a beefy, heavy-jowled professional, striding slowly and majestically down the fairway. Dai Rees played his usual confident game, never afraid to go for the hole, and his 69 gave him the joint lead with Eric Brown and Syd Scott. There were no real surprises at this stage.

On the Thursday, with forty-seven near enough to be in contention and the weather again beautiful, the bunching continued and very few fell back. But poor Dai Rees had one of those days when he was at odds with himself, his clubs and the course, and his 79 took him from the joint lead to the maximum score qualifying for Friday's final rounds. By contrast, John Fallon equalled the Old Course record with a 67 and shot to joint second on 140, a shot behind Thomson whose 68 placed him ominously in the lead along with Eric Brown and Smaildon of Cardiff. Locke with a 69 kept the leaders well in sight. Certainly he could make up four shots in two rounds; and yet this 1955 Open has been described as comparatively colourless, because so many had a feeling in their bones that Thomson would triumph. But he had much to do before that happened.

Remembering that Fallon and Jowle were 17 and 16 years older than Thomson respectively, they put up a tremendous fight over that gruelling final 36 holes. After the third round, Jowle's 69 kept him well in the hunt, one behind Thomson, two ahead of Brown, Weetman and Jacobs, three ahead of Locke and Fallon. It was Fallon who set the target in the final round, going to the turn in a splendid 31. But that lethal 'you never know' of the Old Course asserted itself once more. A weak tee-shot at the eleventh found Strath bunker, and, as Fallon said later,

John Panton in determined mood. A fine player in a wind. *Evening Telegraph*, Dundee.

he could have cheerfully murdered whoever left a deep heelmark where his ball fell. Two of the four shots that he had made up on Thomson were lost at that hole, and although he did have a brave three at the twelfth, there were three fives to follow, and his 283 did not seem quite good enough. Jowle dropped three shots in succession from the twelfth with 5, 5, 6 and came third on 284. But Thomson, knowing about Fallon's 31 out, was playing his usual cheerful but determined game. He had one setback, at the fifth where a bunker cost him a six, but he was out in 35 and on target. Yet one onlooker at the ninth noted that his holing of a short putt there was less than convincing. He must have known that he needed to come back in 37. There was a brief stutter when he was caught in the Beardies at the fourteenth and thereafter in the Grave and it was a seven. Splendid temperament was needed now. There was an almost casual three at the fifteenth: a drive, an approach and a twelve-foot putt; a near three at the sixteenth and a safe 5, 4 finish placed him on 281. He had three-putted only once in the four rounds, at the fifth in the third round. There was one man left with a very slim chance –

The crowd lining the first fairway as Faulkner and Conrad play. *Evening Telegraph*, Dundee.

Henry Cotton in relaxed mood.
Dundee Courier.

Cotton and Thomson, champions with twenty years between them, are paired. St. Andrews University, Cowie Collection.

Peter Thomson in action.

Peter Thomson leaves the last green as Open Champion for the second time. His wife is wearing his first, 1954 medal.

Peter Thomson, five times winner, this time with the trophy at St. Andrews in 1955.
Dundee Courier.

Christie O'Connor. Six under fours on the fourteenth tee, he had a very sad eight, but characteristically he managed a 71 despite that.

Peter Thomson had thoroughly earned his second successive Championship. Yet some sections of the Press have always tended to 'praise him with faint damns'. Of course, he was never such a personality as Jones, Hagen or Locke; he concentrated his energies on playing golf, and that seldom resulted in good copy for the newspapers. He is a highly intelligent man who, in the Press tent, gave clear incisive answers to worthwhile questions but was obviously annoyed by the trivial ones. His book *This Wonderful World of Golf,* with Desmond Zwar, was written because Thomson felt that the only way of answering the worthwhile questions properly was to take Zwar with him for a full year as he played in tournaments all over the world.

CHAPTER 21

A RAPID RETURN TO ST. ANDREWS: 1957 – BOBBY LOCKE

THE OPEN CHAMPIONSHIP was to have been staged at Muirfield in 1957, but political developments necessitated a switch. What a familiar ring that has today. Anthony Eden, who had at last succeeded Churchill as Premier in 1955, ran into trouble less than a year later. It was in late July 1956 that Colonel Nasser, Egypt's Head of State, nationalised the Suez Canal Company in which the British Government had been a principal stockholder since 1875. This action led to an Anglo-French attack on Egypt on 5th November, whereupon Eden was accused of flouting the United Nations, alienating the United States, risking a third world war and bungling the military operations. After several serious illnesses, Eden was still in poor health, and on this ground he resigned in early January 1957. But before that the Open Championship was seen to be in jeopardy. In late November 1956, it had been announced that petrol rationing would be imposed from 17th December, with private motoring restricted to 200 miles a month, and public transport was to be cut. Clearly, Muirfield was far too inaccessible now for the R&A's Championship Committee and their many contractors – not to mention the public.

At this time Beeching's 'axe' had not decimated the railway network; and St. Andrews was on this splendid link with the rest of the United Kingdom. But the Old Course was suffering from the effects of a prolonged drought in the summer and autumn of 1955, followed by the cold, dry spring of 1956. In October 1956, *Golf Monthly*, under the heading 'Decline of the Old Course', carried a recently announced decision to give the famous links a five months' rest during the coming winter. Could the Open be switched there from Muirfield? There must have been monsoonlike rain at times between November 1956 and the end of January 1957 because February's *Golf Monthly* had 'St. Andrews' instead of 'Muirfield' as the Open venue.

Bobby Locke had defeated Reggie Whitcombe in the first-ever televised match, in 1939; and seventeen years later, in 1956, only highlights of the Championship were transmitted. Now, in 1957, the event was given proper television coverage. This provided some drama at the climax of the Championship; but, far more important, it became clear that unless tubular grandstands were installed, and other attractive facilities provided, very few would prefer to travel to the course when they could see far more from their armchairs.

After the two qualifying rounds no-one of any real note had failed, and as Frank Moran put it, 'the cards of the two days are now worthless as your Nasser-dictated petrol coupons'; so by July 1957 rationing had ended.

St. Andrews 1957. Henry Cotton on the 1st tee at the start of a practice round. St. Andrews University,
Cowie Collection.

After the first two rounds of the Championship proper there were twelve within four shots of the lead, in this order: Eric Brown – 139; Flory van Donck – 140; Bobby Locke – 141; Bruce Crampton – 141; Antonio Cerda – 142; John Fallon - 142; Peter Thomson – 142; Laurie Ayton – 143; Cary Middlecoff – 143; John Panton – 143; Mr W.D. Smith – 143; K.A. Macdonald – 143. For the first time in an Open Championship the leaders were to be sent out last in pairs for Friday's final rounds. All this time the weather had been good. On the Friday it was just as warm and Locke, a portly figure in black and white, liked it and took full advantage with a 68; and Thomson's 70 and Brown's 73 left them tied three shots behind. Effectively the race was now between these three, although no praise is high enough for Mr W.D. Smith with his 72, followed by a final 71. Perhaps the best way of highlighting his achievement is to point out that only Eric Brown of Britain's Ryder Cup Team which defeated the United States in that year at Lindrick was ahead of 'Dick' Smith in the final tally. Eric Brown's unfortunate remarks during this and several other Opens should be forgotten. He was a tremendous match player,

Mr W. D. Smith of Selkirk and Prestwick, 71, 72, 72, 71.

Eric Brown, winner of the Vardon Trophy, 1957.

Gary Player on the 1st tee. *Left*: Peter Thomson. *Right*: from left to right: Bernard Hunt, David Thomas and John Jacobs. In plus-fours is Jack McLean, former Scottish Amateur Champion, and runner-up in the U.S. Amateur in 1936 when he was stymied out of 1st place by Johnny Fischer. *Evening Telegraph*, Dundee.

head to head, nothing like so effective in foursomes. In four consecutive Ryder Cup matches between 1953 and 1959 he won all his singles, defeating Lloyd Mangrum, Jerry Barber, Tommy Bolt and Cary Middlecoff. That is worth remembering.

In the final round of the 1957 Open it transpired that Peter Thomson would have needed a 67 to tie with Locke; but they both had excellent 70s. For once, Thomson missed several six-foot putts – and that made all the difference. Brown's 71 took him into third place. The only testing moment for Locke came at the fourteenth where he had lost ground several times in previous Championships. Now he was bunkered in three at the front of the green, but recovered

Bobby Locke, now a portly figure in black and white.

Bobby Locke lines up his putt for a birdie three on the last green to win the 1957 Open. Bruce Crampton watches. *Dundee Courier.*

Locke congratulated by runner-up Peter Thomson. *Evening Telegraph*, Dundee.

In 1958 Bobby Jones was to receive from Provost Robert Leonard the freedom of the city of St. Andrews. Jones died in 1968. A further mark of honour was the memorial service to him in Holy Trinity Church, St. Andrews at which the black-draped silver club, normally reserved for Captains' funerals, was carried in procession and Roger Wethered read the lesson.

brilliantly to get his five. He was virtually home and dry. There was one more piece of drama. His second shot to the eighteenth was splendid, about three feet left of the pin. Nowadays he would have walked up and marked his ball in any case; but in 1957 it was his playing partner, Bruce Crampton, who asked him to mark it, a putter-head's length off Crampton's line. But Locke, perhaps in the excitement of the moment, replaced his ball that putter-head's length from its proper spot. Television brought this to the attention of many viewers, yet no journalist remarked on it in his report. With 36 holes on the Friday, the deadline for reaching Saturday's papers was very tight indeed. When their attention was drawn to the incident the Championship Committee took very little time to decide that, with a three-stroke lead and virtually the same putt from either spot, Locke should not be penalised. John Glover, the Rules Secretary, has pointed out that Dobereiner in his *Book of Golf Disasters* recorded that the Committee's decision was given 'in equity and the spirit of the game', and that Locke, seeking a daily reminder of their compassion, never wore his trademark plus-fours again.

CHAPTER 22

NAGLE'S PUTTING DECISIVE: THE CENTENARY OPEN, 1960

W*HEN ARNOLD PALMER CAME IN 1960* to compete for the first time in our Open Championship it was as reigning U.S. Open Champion. Both his power and his putting were known to be tremendous. In winning that U.S. Open he had started the final round seven behind Mike Souchak, birdied six of the first seven holes in his 30 on the first nine, and gone on to win with a 65. Phenomenal putting had played its part in that victory; and time and again it had proved, and would continue to prove, decisive. It is ironic then that Kel Nagle should have outgunned him on the greens at St. Andrews. Palmer would win the next two Opens, at Birkdale and Troon, and beyond any doubt it was his presence at our Open from1960 onwards that began the revival of its great reputation, a reputation built up down the years until the early 1930s, and then gradually lost.

In 1960 besides Palmer, Sam Snead and Bob Rosburg the American PGA Champion were both entered, but eventually scratched. Two very welcome Americans did arrive: the 76-year-old 1921 Champion, Jock Hutchison, and Gene Sarazen, now 58, the 1932 Champion. They acquitted themselves nobly. Hutchison had intended to play a token nine holes, but was going so well that he completed the round, in 82. Sarazen had a splendid 69 round the Old Course, a 72 round the New, and, honour satisfied, scratched from the Championship proper, explaining that if only he could have a new pair of legs he would still be in contention. The field was very strong: Gary Player, the holder, led the qualifiers, and as well as Palmer there were Thomson and Locke, Christie O'Connor, highly fancied until he took 80 in the first round proper, the 39-year-old, Kel Nagle of Australia, and Roberto de Vicenzo, at this time a naturalised Mexican. Joe Carr had already shown his quality with a 68 round the Old, and in the third round he would break the Amateur record with a 67. Peter Alliss had a record 66 on the Old when qualifying, but sadly did not make the cut for the final two rounds.

The highlight of the first round proper was de Vicenzo's 67 compiled in ideal conditions; by the afternoon Thomson, Palmer and Player had to struggle against a strong breeze which made scoring two or three shots more difficult. Palmer's 70 and the others' 72s left them well placed; but Nagle had a 69, his putter playing the major part, never more than at the Road Hole where he looked likely to take five but holed a forty-footer up the bank from near the wall. Significantly, Palmer had gone for an eight yard putt there and missed the one back, a two-shot swing; that hole had not finished with Palmer yet. After Thursday's round, two overseas players had taken a very definite lead, but not the ones expected to do so. De Vicenzo with two 67s, and Nagle with a second round 67, were on 134 and 136 respectively. Palmer and Thomson were trailing at 141. The question everyone was asking was whether de Vicenzo and at that point to a lesser extent, Nagle, could hold off the challenge that was

St. Andrews 1960, the Centenary Open, Arnold Palmer with former Walker Cup player Leonard
Crawley. *Dundee Courier.*

bound to come from those immediately behind. Nagle had a good reputation among Australians as a 'front runner', of playing well in the lead. In that second round, Palmer had had 34 putts, missing one of under a yard at the seventeenth; Nagle had 31.

On what should have been the final day, Friday, Nagle moved out in front with a 71 despite a six at the fourteenth, and went two shots in front of de Vicenzo who drove out of bounds at the fourteenth on the way to a seven and a disastrous 75. They holed out at the last in the nick of time, because just then there was a tremendous cloudburst and within minutes the course was flooded. Earlier, Palmer's 70 finishing with two fives had left him four shots off the pace. But now the scene was reminiscent of that 1910 Open when conditions had also become farcical. John Jacobs and Bert Williamson were putting on the first green at the start of what should have been their final round, but when the cloudburst hit them the hole was

Eric Brown watches Bernard Hunt drive from the 10th. At 3rd equal, Hunt was to be the leading British player in the 1960 Open. St. Andrews University, Cowie Collection.

Scenes following the July 1960 cloudburst. St. Andrews University, Cowie Collection.

suddenly under water, and putting was out of the question. Threequarters of an inch fell in half an hour, the equivalent of two months' rainfall in the summer of 1959. With the tide nearing full, drains could not cope with the flood; they were particularly ineffective on the Scores so that water raced down past the Clubhouse and on down the Clubhouse steps before flooding the Valley of Sin to a depth of at least three feet. When the Fire Brigade arrived just before five o'clock it took them nearly an hour to pump it out. There was nothing for it but to hold over the final round until the Saturday, however inconvenient that was as regards accommodation for Friday night and long-standing travel arrangements.

On Saturday morning, both Palmer and Nagle were out in 34: Palmer in spite of average putting, Nagle with two gallant savers at the eighth and ninth. At the thirteenth and fifteenth Palmer got back two of the four he was behind. Then for the first time Palmer had a four at the seventeenth; but this was where the title was won and lost. As Nagle studied an awkward eight-footer a huge roar told him that Palmer had got a birdie at the eighteenth, and the strain on him intensified. Nagle's ball rolled slowly up, hesitated, and then to his visible relief just

The crowd check the scoreboard after the cancellation of play on the Friday owing to the cloudburst. *Evening Telegraph*, Dundee.

Kel Nagle and Roberto de Vicenzo shake hands as they leave the 18th green. They finished just
ahead of the cloudburst. St. Andrews University, Cowie Collection.

toppled in. With the milling crowd pressing in on him and under great mental strain his chip to
three feet at the last was heroic, and he made sure that his downhill putt was dead. He had
achieved a new record aggregate of 278.

Never again have Britain and Ireland's amateurs put up such a splendid performance in
the Open Championship: Guy Wolstenholme 283; Joe Carr 285; David Blair 286; Reid Jack 288.
The only British professional ahead of Wolstenholme and Carr was Bernard Hunt.

Just as Braid received an extra gold medal in 1910, in 1960 Nagle received a miniature replica of the Golf Champion Trophy. *Dundee Courier.*

The presentation of the Trophy to Kel Nagle, whose putting had proved decisive. On the extreme right sits the runner-up, Arnold Palmer. St. Andrews University, Cowie Collection.

To mark the centenary of the British Open, Arnold Palmer handed over the scroll which he had brought with him from America. In the left background is Gary Player. *Evening Telegraph, Dundee.*

Joe Carr (285) and Guy Wolstenholme (283) on the 2nd fairway. The only British professional ahead of the amateur pair was Bernard Hunt (282). *Dundee Courier*.

Henry Cotton and Gene Sarazen pictured at the Centenary Dinner. St. Andrews University, Cowie Collection.

At the Centenary Dinner, Willie Auchterlonie, at 88 the oldest living British Open Champion, meets Gary Player, the youngest. St. Andrews University, Cowie Collection.

CHAPTER 23

CHAMPAGNE FOR LEMA: ST. ANDREWS, 1964

*A*NTHONY DAVID LEMA ARRIVED FOR THE 1964 OPEN CHAMPIONSHIP with highly impressive credentials. He had won three of his last four tournaments, and had just beaten Arnold Palmer in a sudden-death play-off for the Cleveland Open. Palmer for his part decided not to come. His aim had been to achieve the Grand Slam: the U.S. and the British Opens, the Masters and the PGA; but, very tired, he had finished weakly in fifth place in the U.S. Open, and decided to have a rest.

Lema was a quite remarkable personality. His first professional appointment had been at a nine hole course in Elko, Nevada, a gambling community of 6,000, with three casinos and two nightclubs. It was a very unusual environment for a future champion. Lema acquired a taste for the bright lights there, and that militated against his developing his talents fully. Then one day he heard Palmer on the radio, explaining his dynamic approach to the game: 'I see what I have to do, and decide that I'll do it. If I have a long putt I think only of making it and shut out the idea of missing it, and of any further putting.' That sorted Lema out. His own approach to golf became very determined indeed; but he retained his generous, sunny Portuguese temperament.

Tip Anderson, who usually caddied for Palmer, had done so for Bruce Devlin of Australia in the qualifying rounds; but he had been paid off on the Saturday night, and hoped to be

Tony Lema in action.

145

Spectators rush to help as the large refreshment marquee is battered by gale-force winds, July 1964.
St. Andrews University, Cowie Collection.

engaged by Lema who had arrived only that day, in company with Nicklaus. That Lema did engage him was a very important factor in his success; no champion before or since had left himself time for fewer than two full practice rounds on the Old Course. For this Championship they could use either the American 1.68 or the British 1.62 ball. Lema played the smaller ball throughout, and said that he would certainly take some back to the States with him.

For the first round proper there was a strong south-west wind which freshened to a gale gusting to around 60 m.p.h. and making the Old Course almost unplayable for those going out later. Christie O'Connor, a great bad-weather golfer, and the French Champion Jean Garaialde were early starters, but even so their 71s were near miraculous. O'Connor had a run of 3, 3, 4, 3, 3, 3, 3, from the seventh to the thirteenth. His putt had appeared to stop on the lip at the twelfth, but several seconds later the wind toppled it in. Lema's 73 was helped by an early start and a sixteen yard putt at the last. His wedge play was magnificent throughout; but especially in this first round he showed equal skill with the shot he had newly acquired, the pitch and run. Nicklaus had a very brave 76 much later in the day, and declared that these were the worst conditions he had ever met. Poor Bob Charles, the holder, had a 79, as did Peter

Tony Lema with caddie Tip Anderson, without whom he said he wouldn't have won.

Lema on the last green on the way to his closing 70. With him is Frenchman Garaialde. *Evening Telegraph*, Dundee.

Thomson, who said that the putter shook in his hands and the ball moved. At the height of the storm, Eric Brown was short with two well-struck woods at the first, a distance of only 367 yards; he took 80. Many competitors were sorry for once that the crowds were kept to the side of the fairways. Had they been allowed to follow the players they would have provided some protection from the wind, especially on the greens.

In the second round conditions had improved; the wind had dropped to around 30 m.p.h.. Even so only one man broke 70, and Tony Lema had only 33 putts in his 68. Nicklaus had 40 in his 76, more than he had ever taken since turning professional. One great favourite emerged during the second day's play: Lu Liang Huan - Mr Lu - weighing less than nine stones, went to the turn against the wind in 33 and had an excellent 71. Christie O'Connor had his putter to thank for a 73, which he said could easily have been an 80. Garaialde was philosophical about his 74: 'Better weather, worse score – but that's golf.' Eric Brown, out in the eye of the first-round storm, failed by three shots to qualify for the final rounds and was justifiably aggrieved. This time there were no amateurs among the qualifiers for Friday's play,

On the Friday morning Nicklaus, nine behind Lema, had a record-breaking 66 – but Lema's second successive 68 meant that the gap remained seven. Lema had started badly and as he walked up the sixth fairway three over fours he could see that Nicklaus coming down the thirteenth was then five under. Lema thought, as he said later, 'Here it goes again'. But he covered the last thirteen holes in seven under fours with a splendid succession of five threes round the Loop, and he finished 3, 4, 4, 3. By contrast, Weetman and Faulkner, the 1951 Champion, fell away badly with 75 and 80 respectively. Only Bernard Hunt kept going with a fine 70. Roberto de Vicenzo underlined his quality also with a 70 and his closing 67 gave him third place. That meant that in eight attempts to that point he had been second once and third five times. Now forty, he was still clearly capable of winning – and he did so in 1967 at Hoylake, to everyone's delight.

In the final round it was far from a close-run thing. Nicklaus's 40 putts in the second round had left him too much to do against a player of Lema's calibre. With a five at the fourth and a six at the fifth, Nicklaus added a 68 to his morning 66. As he began that final round, he had watched Lema holing a curly twenty-footer on the last green for his three, and throwing back his head raised his arms to high heaven, as if to say, 'What can you do against this sort of golf?' Lema's closing 70 was compiled in an atmosphere of almost unnatural calm. He was seven shots ahead with nine holes to go, and never for a moment looked like having a really disastrous hole from that point on. At the eighteenth the huge crowd pressed on so far that they overran Garaialde's ball and ten minutes elapsed before the Frenchman could play his second shot. Lema's second, appropriately a delicate pitch and run, seemed almost to coincide with the crowd's engulfing him: as he said later, 'I was hit four times before I completed my follow through'. When he struggled to the green it was to see his ball less than two feet from the pin – his third three out of four. When he reached the Press Tent he told them, 'If you wanna talk to me you'd better yell for I'm right up on cloud 9'.

Lema was following in the footsteps of Densmore Shute, Sam Snead and Ben Hogan all of whom won the Open at their first appearance. Any great course however unaccustomed and subtle will yield to a great player if – and it is a very big 'if' – he has a really great caddie. In this case, Tip Anderson had carried the clubs of three out of the last four Open Champions. Lema was full of praise for him: 'It was amazing how often he put the right club in my hand; I

'Champagne' Tony Lema. St. Andrews University, Cowie Collection.

would be stretching it if I said I did 50 per cent of it.' He was generous in quite a different way to the Press, to the tune of twenty cases of champagne.

Golf lost not only a great golfer but one of its most endearing personalities just two years later when tragically, in July 1966, he and his wife were killed in a 'plane crash on their way to a tournament.

CHAPTER 24

1970 – FOR SANDERS DISASTER, FOR NICKLAUS TRIUMPH

EVERY DOG HAS ITS DAY, and in August, 1956 I was delighted when playing in the Elie Links Championship in a tremendous blatter of wind and rain to finish the first of the two rounds just one shot behind the 72 recorded by W. Dickson Smith, who came fifth equal in the Open at St. Andrews the following year. Further, he had been quite pleased with his 72. As a result I was sent out in the afternoon with 'Dick' Smith and since he was such a distinguished player about 70 or 80 spectators braved all that wind and rain to watch. He was a very long hitter indeed and I can recall that he was on the 450 yard ninth with a drive and a nine iron. He was marvellous to play with, tremendously kind and – low be it spoken – even gave me some very useful advice on one occasion. As a result I staggered in runner-up.

Now what has this to do with Nicklaus? Three years later I was at the Walker Cup match in 1959 at Muirfield and along with many others had my first glimpse of him. When I arrived on that Saturday it was to find that 'Dick' Smith was chipping on from about forty yards short of the seventeenth green – this man rated a very long hitter – and I could see a ball six yards behind the pin and a very sturdily built, fair-haired, crewcut college boy advancing to it; and this was Jack Nicklaus. After being runner-up in the 1964 Open to Lema, he had been even more sturdily built in the later 1960s; but now in 1970 he had lost 28 pounds by following a very strict diet. He had found himself tiring badly in that tied Ryder Cup match in 1969 when he was for once required to play 36 holes a day, and applied the obvious remedy. It was all part of his build-up – or should I say build-down? – to the 1970 Open because, as he said on arrival, 'If you want to be a player who is remembered you've got to win at St. Andrews. All the famous players have won at St. Andrews.'

There had been many changes in and around the Old Course since 1964. No longer did the trains rumble past players putting on the fifteenth and sixteenth greens, although the out of bounds fence remained. Where the stationmaster's garden and the black sheds had been there was now a modern hotel, decidedly not to everyone's taste, especially Henry Longhurst's who declared that it looked like a chest-of-drawers with drawers pulled out. Subsequently, enlarged again and again, it has become vital to the survival of St. Andrews as an Open Championship venue. For the first time also there was a large stand behind the eighteenth green, an even bigger one down the right-hand side of the first fairway, and a small one on the right-hand side of the eighteenth. Seven other stands out on the Course meant that in all there was free accommodation for over 10,000 spectators. The tented village had grown considerably, forcing the R&A to site part of it on the Jubilee Course quite far from the Clubhouse. Television coverage was the biggest yet: all in colour, thirteen cameras were to show play on two thirds of the course, the first six and the last six holes. The famous Loop with the only two short

A scene from 1967. The Old Course Hotel is under construction and the 17th tee, wide out left, provides an easier drive. *Dundee Courier.*

holes, the eighth and the eleventh, would not be in range of television. Four low-level cameras were placed so as to give virtually an eye-level view of the play at several strategic points, notably of the putting on the seventeenth green.

For the first round, conditions at the start were perfect: virtually no wind, and the greens made placid by earlier rain. As a result there were 21 scores of 70 or better – but later in the day with two-thirds of the field in the Clubhouse, there was a cloudburst such as had washed out play in 1910 and more recently in 1960. Those safely in were headed by Neil Coles's record 65, Horton on 66, and, lurking in a pack at 68, Nicklaus, Palmer, Sanders and Peter

Great clubmaker Laurie Auchterlonie pictured in 1967. He and his father Willie spanned over 50 years as Honorary Professionals to the R&A . St. Andrews University, Cowie Collection.

Open Champions gathered for the 1970 event. Back row left to right – Arthur Havers, Gene Sarazen, Dick Burton, Fred Daly, Roberto de Vicenzo, Arnold Palmer, Kel Nagle, Bobby Locke, Henry Cotton, and Peter Thomson. Front row – Densmore Shute, Bob Charles, Max Faulkner, Jack Nicklaus, Tony Jacklin and Gary Player. Photo: Ian Joy, St. Andrews.

Thomson. The news from the course was sensational: the holder, Tony Jacklin, had reached the turn in 29, starting with three birdies, with two more at the seventh and eighth, and an eagle two at the ninth where he holed a full wedge. He was eight under 4s on the twelfth tee but could see the storm clouds gathering and wondered if he would be able to complete his round. Soon there was thunder rumbling in the distance, and by the time he came to play his second at the fourteenth, reachable with a three wood, the rain had started. At the top of his swing someone shouted 'Fore!', causing Jacklin to push it far right into a gorse bush and unplayable almost green high. The hole was under water by the time he reached his ball, and after an agonising wait he learned that all completed rounds would count; he was one of 38

Tony Jacklin at the 1970 Open. Eight under 4s on the twelfth tee, he could hear thunder rumbling in the distance. At the fourteenth he had to mark his ball and return on the Thursday. By then the magic was gone. *Evening Telegraph*, Dundee.

who would mark their balls and return at 7.30 am on the Thursday. By then the magic had gone, there was now a stiff breeze, and he struggled to a 67.

To his great credit he managed a 70 later that day and was one shot behind Trevino but level with Nicklaus. Coles and Sanders were two shots further back. Trevino was untroubled by the now shifting and scurrying wind, accustomed as he was to this kind of thing in Texas. Jacklin was annoyed with himself for not adapting swiftly enough to the different conditions on the Thursday morning. Peter Oosterhuis matched the best over the last 63 holes; but his opening 39 to the turn, ten worse than Jacklin, left him too much to do.

There was little change in the leading positions after the third round. Trevino had a two stroke lead over Jacklin, Sanders and Nicklaus. This time Palmer had failed to charge; his 76 left him eight behind Trevino. No one could have guessed at this point quite how dramatic the contest would become from now on. For his part, Doug Sanders, a well-known lover of the

Sanders driving. If, like him, you have a short, quick backswing, then your master eye is your right one.

The final round: Sanders salvages a heroic 4 out of the Road Bunker. *Dundee Courier.*

The notorious missed putt on the 18th. Said Henry Longhurst: 'There but for the grace of God . . .'

bright lights, was complaining humorously on that Friday night that he had not been himself all week, going to bed early instead of sampling the pleasures of night life in St. Andrews. Today he had had a tartan edge to his clothing; on the morrow he promised it would not be, 'jeans and tennis shoes!'

The final round was disastrous for both Trevino and Jacklin. In windy conditions, the Mexican was spraying shots right and left, so that he had long putts on several of these vast greens, and failed to get down in two on five occasions. Out in 40, he had in fact to finish 4, 4, 4, 3, for his 77. Sanders, with whom he was paired, was much slower and more deliberate than Trevino, by nature a fast player, and this cannot have helped. Jacklin's chances were rated highly; he was usually particularly good in a wind, but somehow the usual inspiration was lacking. The end came at the sixteenth when, going for a three, he three putted. The battle was now between Sanders and Nicklaus, who had started level. Nicklaus, out in 35 was one ahead, only to take four to Sanders' three at the eleventh; and when Nicklaus bogeyed the sixteenth, Sanders was at last in the lead. He salvaged a heroic four out of the Road Bunker, and hit a fine drive perhaps fifty yards short of the green at the last. A four would do it. His pitch downwind was decidedly strong, a good twelve yards past the flag, and, as Henry Longhurst said, 'It's not over yet'. His first putt left him that dreaded three-footer, breaking from left to right, to win the Open. As Sanders said later: 'I was over the ball and when I looked down I thought I saw a spot of sand in the line. Without changing the position of my feet I bent

Sanders walks off the last green. *Evening Telegraph*, Dundee.

Nicklaus and Sanders had tied for a Sunday play-off. Here, on the eve, they hold the Trophy between them. *Dundee Courier*.

The play-off. With an awesome drive Jack Nicklaus played through the eighteenth green and up the bank, in a similar position to the one shown here. *Dundee Courier.*

down to pick it up. It was a piece of brown grass. I didn't take the time to move away and get re-organized. I mis-hit the ball – hit it in the neck of the face – and pushed it to the right of the hole.'

The play-off was over 18 holes instead of 36, for the first time since the Open became a 72 hole Championship in 1892. Nicklaus on the fourteenth tee was four ahead and seemingly bound to win; but Sanders holed a longer putt than Nicklaus missed at the fourteenth, had a birdie at the fifteenth and came within a single shot of the lead when for the second successive time Nicklaus took five at the sixteenth. The seventeenth was halved splendidly in four. How ironic it was that this time Sanders played the eighteenth perfectly, laying his second a yard from the hole. It was here that Nicklaus peeled off his sweater and hit that huge drive through the green and up the bank. A chip to eight feet left him a firmer putt than Sanders had had the previous day, and as the television pictures show, his ball caught the right-hand lip of the hole, spun left and dropped in. His spontaneous reaction of hurling his putter in the air and nearly braining Sanders revealed what a release of tension can do. Sanders shook hands and then holed a putt of the length that had so tragically defeated him on the Saturday

opposite page
Willie Whitelaw makes the presentation to Nicklaus. Sanders looks on. *Evening Telegraph*, Dundee.

Nicklaus has won. Instinctively throwing his putter in the air to release the tension, he comes near to braining Sanders.

CHAPTER 25

1978: NICKLAUS – AGAIN!

S OMEONE ONCE SAID 'Experience is everything at St. Andrews', and with hindsight it is easy to see that in 1978 Nicklaus had a huge advantage over Watson in that respect. At Turnberry the year before, their tremendous battle over the last two rounds was quite different; neither had had previous experience of the course. That marvellous seven-iron 178 yards downwind at the final hole from Watson to about two feet from the flag, which brought from Peter Alliss the inspired 'Elementary my dear Watson!' was made with Watson's heels in divots filled with sand and to a very hard green. There had to be an element of luck. Now, at St. Andrews, Watson had never played the Old Course before, was arriving in time for about four practice rounds and had to get used to the time change. Nicklaus as he explained later had arrived the previous week when 'few of the guys were here and didn't get to experience'

The scene is set for 1978. *Dundee Courier.*

Watched by Graham Marsh, Arnold Palmer tees off with all his usual power. *Dundee Courier.*

in advance the complete change of wind direction on the fourth and final day. Raymond Floyd had arrived with Nicklaus, so that his marvellous 68 that day was based on local knowledge.

As for Nicklaus, sixteen years in top class golf had taught him to be patient and wait for to come, especially on the Old Course which somehow resents being grabbed by the throat in the Palmer and Watson manner. That was demonstrated in the course of the 1978 Championship. On the eve of it Nicklaus revealed another factor which was strongly in his favour: a few weeks before coming to Britain he had discovered what was wrong with his swing, a flaw which explained his spraying of shots in tournaments in America and his unusually poor season there. It took Jack Grout, his only-ever coach, five visits to spot that Nicklaus had moved his hands on the club about quarter-of-an-inch. As Jack pointed out after his win, he needed only a subtle change in grip: 'It was the key to my tempo to clearing my left side and to not closing at the top.'

The one major change for this Championship was the introduction of the larger ball. That unforgettable moment in 1970 when Nicklaus peeled off his sweater and drove over the back

Lee Trevino slides the ball from left to right in 1978. *Evening Telegraph*, Dundee.

of the 18th green had been possible because the small ball was still in use, and the fairway was much faster.

The honours of the opening day went to Aoki, then 35 and the major winner on the Japanese circuit in 1978 with 34,000,000 yen. He has been described as having the worst-looking golf swing ever seen in a Championship, and his putting technique defies all the rules too. But on that first day he seemed the only one who could hole longish putts, especially the successive par putts of twenty feet at the 17th and 18th for an opening 68. He putts with the toe of the putter tilted up far off the ground because, as he says, 'the sweet spot is in the heel'. Among those one shot behind him was Jack Newton who had lost to Watson in the play-off for the 1975 Carnoustie Open, and now had had to pre-qualify, as had Doug Sanders despite his tremendous performance in 1970.

Oosterhuis, making a very rare appearance in Britain, was felt to have a good chance because wayward drives escape punishment more often at St. Andrews than at most championship circuits – and he is not the straightest of drivers. His two great assets always were his ability to manoeuvre the ball well from the humps, hollows and slopes of links courses, and his beautiful putting. In the event he came quite close to winning.

Seve Ballesteros came in with a very solid 69, but like so many others he bogied the 17th and very quickly pointed out that 'it may be a bogey five to you but it is a par five to me'. Seve was to find the seventeenth disastrous the very next day. But now its first real victim was Brian Barnes, the massive Scot whose chief claim to fame must be that in the 1975 Ryder Cup on American soil he had defeated Jack Nicklaus twice in one day. At three under par and on the front of the 17th green in two, Barnes was splendidly placed; but the pin was sited perilously close behind the Road Bunker. There can only have been an inch in it but Barnes found the bunker, exploded out past the pin and took six. As he said later, 'I made a fool of myself through being too greedy, too damned clever . . . I should have settled for a safety first putt finishing maybe seven feet away.' He felt 71 in the morning conditions was 'pitiful'.

Tom Watson's 73 was marred only by his six at the fourteenth but he was playing very confidently and seemed in no way worried by the eccentricities of a course he had played so seldom. The fourteenth claimed one other distinguished victim, Lanny Wadkins, who put two out of bounds off the tee and did wonderfully well to salvage an eight by getting down in two shots from Hell Bunker.

By the time Nicklaus started in the early afternoon any fears that the course would be taken apart had vanished. The greens were almost perfect – there were no complaints all week – but of course their size is a problem in itself. In 1970 someone had had the temerity to suggest that Jack's second shots were being left too far from the pin, to be met with a pugnacious 'Have YOU ever played this course?' On the answer 'Yes', Nicklaus continued,

Tom Watson approaching the eighteenth green.

Ben Crenshaw is watched by Neil Coles. Coles had a record 65 (which still stands) in 1970.
Crenshaw was to finish joint runner-up in 1978 with Simon Owen, Raymond Floyd and Tom Kite.
Evening Telegraph, Dundee.

'Then you'll appreciate that it's not always as easy as it looks here to work the ball close to the hole'. Like Watson, he was playing when the wind was strong enough to be a factor; the second half was longer and the pin placements at the front of the greens on the way out were more difficult. So his 71 along with Palmer, Coles and Peter McEvoy was highly acceptable. What a year McEvoy had: a successful defence of his Amateur title, first Amateur in the Open, and, perhaps toughest of all, competing in all four rounds of the Masters at Augusta.

Nick Faldo, at twenty the reigning PGA Champion, and a Ryder Cup hero in 1977 at Lytham with wins in all three matches, foursomes, four-balls and singles, was well placed from the start and throughout displayed the fighting qualities which have been particularly evident in recent years. Kite and Crenshaw would also do well, but Jacklin and Wadkins were to miss the cut.

On the second day, Thursday, Nicklaus played quite splendid golf from tee to green and had he been able to sink just a few putts would have been several strokes ahead of the field at the end of the day. As it was he had a most frustrating time, needed an average of two putts per green, and finished in 72. Fourteen of his eighteen second putts were within six inches of the hole. He himself commented that he had wasted the Loop, holes seven to twelve, by completing them only in par. He felt he was playing well enough with his adjusted grip 'to shoot any kind of round'. But even on these vast greens 36 putts were far too many.

Raymond Floyd drives at the 17th watched by Peter Oosterhuis and Jack Nicklaus. He was to finish joint runner-up. *Dundee Courier.*

By contrast, Watson took most of his chances with the putter; his wedge play was splendid, and several times left him from two inches to a foot away. His four birdies gave him a 68, and he was joined on a total of 141 by two Japanese, Ozaki and Nakajima. Kite had the same total, and Weiskopf with a par 72 to add to his opening 69 was also three under.

Two strokes ahead of this group, at five under on 139, were Crenshaw and Aoki, a lead which they held in the Clubhouse for a long time; Arnold Palmer was at one stage five under too, and although one of the Beardies cost him a shot at the fourteenth he was still four under standing on the seventeenth tee. Even a 5, 4 finish would put him alongside Watson and the others. The seventeenth had always given Palmer trouble – witness his total of 19 shots to Nagle's 14 there in 1960. Palmer had been in the left rough on the opening day and had taken five. This time he tried to cut it down the right side; it bounced on the road and over the wall, and by way of rough and sand he did well to get a five with his second ball. He was to go out of bounds there again in the next round. 'It may be a famous hole,' said Palmer, 'but I don't like it.' He added, 'I know I should play the hole safely, play for a five – but that's not my way.'

Peter Oosterhuis drives at the 18th tee. In the background is the Old Course Hotel without its subsequent extensions. Henry Longhurst likened it to a chest of drawers with all the drawers left open. *Evening Telegraph*, Dundee.

Some horseplay between Bernard Gallacher and Brian Barnes. *Dundee Courier.*

He underlined his great fighting qualities when he followed that disastrous seven with a beautiful three at the eighteenth.

Late in the day it seemed likely that Ballesteros would gain the outright lead; he was seven under fours on the seventeenth tee. For all his statement on the Wednesday that the hole was a par five to him, he sent his first tee shot out of bounds and, obviously furious, unleashed a second drive far down the middle to within four-iron range, put it on the green, and with two putts had a fine par four; but six it was, he just missed a birdie at the last, and his 69 left him alongside Crenshaw and Aoki. Afterwards, Seve said that the seventeenth was so difficult because of the places they found to put the pin: 'Tomorrow maybe they no put the hole on the green at all . . .!'

For the third day running the weather on the Friday was dull and still early on, followed by sunshine and a rising easterly breeze around noon. At Turnberry the previous year Watson and Nicklaus had shot 65 each on the Friday, and so turned it into more or less a match-play battle between them with the rest nowhere. Now at St. Andrews it became more and more exciting as the top dozen players were separated by only three shots with one round to go. Poor Nakajima had that tragic nine at the seventeenth, and was no longer in the running.

Hubert Green had equalled Gary Cullen's fine 67 of the second day; and a lanky New Zealander, Simon Owen, did likewise to join Nicklaus on 212, a shot behind Watson and Oosterhuis. Nicklaus's 69 had included three putts at the eighth from no distance at all. He put it down to a helicopter which with its totally different sound from crowd noises was the one thing which could really upset his concentration. Crenshaw and Aoki were also on 212, and still very much in contention were Faldo, Weiskopf, Kite and the near-veteran Peter Thomson.

It was on the Saturday that the wind swung round completely, producing difficulties reflected in the scores of those who had not previously encountered these conditions: Watson 76; Weiskopf 75; Oosterhuis and Aoki 73. Kite and Crenshaw hung on well with 70 and 71 respectively – but Floyd's 68 brought him level with them, his experience in the previous week invaluable. The battle was now between the pairing of Nicklaus and Owen. After a nervy start the New Zealander had played very well, and by the fifteenth they were on level terms. Nicklaus was much nearer the pin with a good birdie chance, but when Owen chipped in

Brian Barnes and Jack Nicklaus watched by a large gallery. This was to be Nicklaus's Open, but in a Ryder Cup encounter Barnes had the distinction of beating Nicklaus twice in one day.
Evening Telegraph, Dundee.

Simon Owen smiles bravely in defeat.

from 25 yards, Nicklaus just failed to match that three. Suddenly Owen was at seven under and one ahead. But like any great champion, Nicklaus struck back at once. His three wood at the sixteenth left him a 9-iron approach to six feet. Owen was further down off the tee but in semi-rough, and his next was well over the back with that horrible shot over the bank. Whether he had had a flier – as Nicklaus thought possible – or the adrenalin had flowed too freely, who can say? Owen now elected to putt it; and off a downslope with the pin near the back of the green there was little chance of getting it near any other way. Almost inevitably the ball went to the top of the bank and slid back. He was down in two more, but Nicklaus holed for his three, a two shot swing and the lead. When he followed that with a safe drive, a six-iron to the front of the seventeenth green and putted up dead it was nearly all over; Owen had found the road and took five. But to his great credit after two very sad holes, he made a tie still possible by putting his approach at the last eight feet away; for Nicklaus was more than ten yards from

Jack Nicklaus, British Open Golf Champion (again), 1978. *Evening Telegraph*, Dundee.

Tension over, Nicklaus and caddie Jimmie Dickinson let victory sink in. *Dundee Courier*.

Nicklaus was also to have honorary life membership of the St. Andrews Golf Club conferred upon him by Captain George Grant. *Dundee Courier.*

the pin on that treacherous green. In the event he was down in two, and Owen missed. Nicklaus's 69 and Floyd's 68 were not the only scores under 70 that day, but none of the other contenders did as well.

It was Nicklaus's seventeenth victory in the four major championships, and one measure of his calibre was that he had won each of the Grand Slam events three times around while no one else had done it more than once. Perhaps more important in the context of the St. Andrews Opens, he had joined those other immortals, Taylor and Braid, in winning twice in succession here.

CHAPTER 26

THE DECISIVE ROAD HOLE, 1984 – WATSON AND BALLESTEROS

*T*HERE HAS BEEN NO SHORTAGE OF COMMENT about the dreaded seventeenth hole at St. Andrews. Jack Nicklaus has frequently described it as a par four-and-a-half. Trevino reckoned that if you made par at the Road Hole, you were passing up half the field. Henry Cotton snorted that if an architect had designed it they would have wanted their money back. But Watson in 1978, looking from the Old Course Hotel balcony, decided that it was a really great hole and felt that it could provide one of the key shots in that Championship. He was right. Simon Owen found the road and dropped to two shots behind Nicklaus. For poor Watson it was to be one of two key shots in the 1984 Open.

Many wondered whether Nicklaus could win a third St. Andrews Open in succession, a feat as unparalleled as the nineteen Major Championships already to his name. When it was announced that just before the start of the 1984 Open, St. Andrews University would confer on him an honorary degree of Doctor of Laws, it was a fitting tribute from Scotland's oldest university to the game with which it shares a home. Nicklaus was close to tears as he accepted this unique honour. He said that St. Andrews was his favourite place in all the golfing world and added that he still cringed at the thought of the raw, crewcut, over-confident 19-year-old who was sure he could take Muirfield apart when he had come over for the Walker Cup in 1959.

Shortly before the 1984 Open I had had a round on the Old Course, and had noticed many places where a large number of divots had been taken especially about fifty yards short of the tenth green. Of course, it was bound to happen on this municipal course with its huge traffic between April and November. The tees and greens were beautiful. Months later, I asked Michael Bonallack about the divots and whether any top players had complained. His answer was very interesting: 'Never! – a really good player dreads a flier even from semi-rough; he can get stop out of a bad lie on the fairway.'

During the practice rounds for the 1984 Open, Fred Couples demonstrated his power by bouncing his tee shot at the first over the Swilcan to the green – and he then told his caddie off for not mentioning it was there! Over at the seventeenth, some spectators were puzzled because Hal Sutton was practising an unusual shot; he was hitting his ball against the wall at the road and bouncing it back towards the green. This was a tactic first employed successfully by Francis Ouimet, the first American Captain of the Royal and Ancient, in 1951, and in 1988 the first golfer since Bobby Jones to be featured on a postage stamp in the United States.

Once the 1984 Open was underway it was noticeable that the Rules of Golf Committee intended to emphasise the one major change in the 1984 revision of the Rules. They knew that many would be fetching up in the Swilcan Burn, and a Rules man was there to ensure that the

Further honours were to come Jack Nicklaus's way. In 1984 St. Andrews University conferred upon him the honorary degree of Doctor of Laws. *Evening Telegraph*, Dundee.

Jack Nicklaus showing off his honorary degree.

ball was then dropped at arm's length – not over the shoulder.

It is worth recording that before the Championship began, Ian Wood of the *Scotsman* wrote: 'However none of this shilly-shallying. It's Seve Ballesteros for the Open.'

At the end of the first round, three were tying for the lead on 67: Greg Norman, Peter Jacobsen and Bill Longmuir, the Scot who had led the field in the first round at Lytham in 1979. This time he had had an amazing escape from trouble at the Road Hole. Well in the rough on the left off the tee, he had had a flier with a six-wood lent to him by Greg Norman; his ball had sped across the road and hit the wall, and he achieved at long distance what Sutton had been trying, a ricochet to the green. Ian Baker-Finch, who was to have an outstanding Championship, had been practising with his fellow Australians, Peter Thomson and Kel Nagle, and their advice helped him to the first of three excellent rounds, a 68. Faldo, Kite and Ballesteros were on 69. The Spaniard joked about the size of the double greens: 'I have one good score – on the green. A hundred yards from the hole and I get down in two.' Watson was reasonably pleased with his 71, but Nicklaus had a poor 76, and required a par round to make the cut. Bill Rogers, the 1981 Champion, was three times out of bounds at the fourteenth and his 12 there led to an 83.

The leader board at the end of the second day featured almost all of those who had been tipped as possible winners before the Open began: Nick Faldo, Seve Ballesteros, Lee Trevino, Tom Watson, Bernhard Langer, Lanny Wadkins and Tom Kite. Six strokes covered the first dozen. Jack Nicklaus scraped in on 148, but even with his 68 in the third round, many wrote him off as a further Major winner. They had their answer in April, 1986, when Jack won his sixth U.S. Masters title, his twentieth Major in all. But now, three strokes clear of this illustrious field was a remarkable newcomer from Australia, Ian Baker-Finch, at ten under par. When the Press investigated him they found that he was the New Zealand Open Champion and had gained his exemption for the British Open by being in the first six on the Australian Order of

An aerial view of the tented village in 1984. In the centre is the Old Course Hotel with extensions, before more recent reconstruction. *Dundee Courier.*

Jack Nicklaus arrives to do battle.
Evening Telegraph, Dundee.

Another famous arrival: Tom
Watson. *Dundee Courier*.

Seven years on from Turnberry and their famous duel in the sun, there was no head-to-head this time between Watson and Nicklaus. *Evening Telegraph*, Dundee.

Merit. Known to his fellow-Australians variously as 'Sparrow' and 'Hyphen' he was quick to point out that with a name like that his ancestors had not gone to the penal colony! In achieving this halfway total of 134 he had shown splendid fighting qualities especially over the last two holes, getting up and down from the Road bunker at the seventeenth and saving his par at the eighteenth from the Valley of Sin, his final putt being of the dreaded 'Doug Sanders' length. Before the third round began, however, there were some who wondered whether, like Bobby Clampett at Troon in 1982, he might now have shot his bolt.

As has happened several times in the last few years – notably at Sandwich in 1985 and Turnberry in 1986 – the weather had already played a major part and would continue to do so. Those with early starting times had had beautiful weather; but those starting later found it had clouded over, while a chill breeze sprang up off the sea. Tony Jacklin pointed out that with a mid-morning start, followed by a mid-afternoon one, he had found the course formidable. In his second round, Greg Norman followed his opening 67 with a 74, resulting from a run of six

Greg Norman with Ben Crenshaw. Six successive 5s in the second round were to prove fatal to Norman's chances. *Dundee Courier*.

5s in a row from the twelfth, only one of which was a par. He spoke of a lack of 'feel'; perhaps his fingers were numb!

In the course of the third round the overall picture became much clearer. Faldo, perhaps affected by a missed putt of under two feet at the first, fell away rapidly to a miserable 76. When he did manage a birdie at the tenth he celebrated it in ironic style by going into an intricate dance.

Langer came to the fore with some very fine golf, but said rather cynically that although about a hundred thousand Germans might be delighted, 'the other sixty million probably won't be too interested'.

Trevino, after a sparkling 67 in the second round, found the wind a little too much for him when he turned into it and fell back to join Wadkins. Trevino's schedule had been quite remarkably punishing. Earlier in the Open week he had been filming 'The Trevino Connection' which included a good deal of footage shot within the R&A Clubhouse and interviews with Sanders, Palmer and Watson. When I arrived at eight one morning he had been filming from 5 am, and he was back at 7 pm for a further long session. Presumably he was a little less busy while winning the American PGA a few months later.

In compiling his two under par 70, Ballesteros had one thoroughly uncharacteristic shot, a five iron at the short eighth which he mis-hit so badly that he was well left and about fifty yards short. He saved his three with a lovely chip which had to hit one particular spot if it was to finish close.

And what of Baker-Finch? His play during the first nine holes was of the order which had put him ahead of the rest. He birdied the first from eight yards, the fourth from the same distance, and got down in two for his third birdie from about twenty yards at the fifth. He was a little lucky at the ninth to escape with a par after tangling with the Mrs. Kruger bunker and then the heather – eventually holing from three yards. He then stood at thirteen under par; but he had to struggle on the inward nine. A visit to the Beardies at the 14th cost him a bogey six; and for the only time he failed to get his par at the seventeenth, although a five was far more normal than a four. His 71 left him eleven under par.

Meanwhile, Watson had played a quite splendid round of 66, and was also eleven under par after 54 holes. His one bogey had been at the second, sandwiched between two birdies and followed by three more from the fifth to the seventh, to be out in 32. Two more birdies followed, at the tenth and twelfth. He even solved the seventeenth, having had a five and a six thus far. This time he hit a two-iron to the green, and two-putted for a par from twenty-five yards. His 66 moved him from five shots behind, to the joint lead. He now seemed to have a record-tying sixth Open Championship within his reach. Not only could he equal Vardon's record, but with victories already at Carnoustie, Turnberry, Troon and Muirfield he could achieve a unique record of winning an Open on every Scottish course, the Scottish Slam as the Americans call it. Watson was on his game and that is why Langer said on that cooling Saturday afternoon, 'Tom is the man to beat tomorrow'. Ballesteros agreed with him: 'Watson is a great player. He is playing his best now and he's confident. And I think he is the man to beat.' He added one very prophetic remark: 'If I don't par the seventeenth tomorrow, I will come back Monday.' What a Sunday was in prospect!

The field was now down to 63, and there were very few real contenders: Baker-Finch and Watson were on 205; Langer and Ballesteros on 207. There was a five-stroke gap after that to

Consolation for Crenshaw was to come in the shape of a hole-in-one at the 8th on the final day.

Baiocchi, Wadkins and Trevino – and it seemed decidedly too big.

As often, the best scoring on the final day came from those from whom the pressure of winning had been removed. Graham Marsh, Sandy Lyle and Greg Norman all had 67s in the flat calm of the early morning. Norman had two 74s sandwiched between two 67s, the middle pair compiled when the inward half against a cold and blustery wind was ballooning many scores. It would be this kind of experience that equipped Norman to win the 1986 Open at Turnberry, in similar unpleasant conditions, allied to his ability to hit narrow fairways from the tee. Fred Couples and Ken Brown had 68s and among those on 69 were Faldo, Crenshaw and Lanny Wadkins. Faldo was thoroughly dejected: 'Finishing top Briton is nice – but they expect me to do at least that.'

The main focus of attention was to be the two final pairings: Ballesteros and Langer followed by Baker-Finch and Watson. Ballesteros was confident and ready for battle: 'First we beat Langer – then we go after Watson.' Both he and Langer gave very little for Baker-Finch's chances. He had never played with a great American before, except in his imagination. As a boy on his father's avocado farm in Queensland he would aim three balls at various targets. One ball was his own, one was Watson's and one was Nicklaus's. Yet strangely enough on that first tee Watson appeared more tense than he did, asking his caddie, 'Why are you shaking, Alfie?' That first hole was to begin a nightmare for Baker-Finch. Perhaps he betrayed his inexperience when, after a good tee-shot, he played his second just as a distracting roar came from the nearby seventeenth green. His ball hit the green and then to his horror spun back into the Swilcan Burn. His well-saved five there was in sharp contrast to the three of the previous day when he had holed the first of several splendid putts. He was never in contention after that. In fact to achieve a miserable 79 he had to finish 3, 4, 4, 3 – an echo of his brave closes earlier on. Langer playing with Ballesteros had a sad time with his putter missing no fewer than five birdie attempts from around three yards between the second hole and the turn. He admitted afterwards that this had prevented him from worrying the leading pair, although a birdie at long last at the eighteenth tied him for second.

A tremendous battle was developing between Watson and Ballesteros – but one hole apart, compared with the head-to-head between Watson and Nicklaus at Turnberry in 1977. There were two occasions, on the way to a superbly dramatic finish over the last two holes, when Ballesteros might easily have been unsettled. From the sixth tee he hit his drive well left and muttered 'It's in the bunker'. Just then a spectator gave a loud guffaw – probably about something quite different – but Seve rounded on him in a flash with 'You think that's funny?' There was a sudden silence, but Seve had missed the bunker, and a tense moment was past. Then at the short eleventh Langer hit a fine eight-iron to ensure an easy three. Seve also played an eight but was woefully short, and was only just on the green with his second: a four was the result. As he explained later, he had forgotten that Langer had adjusted the loft on his eight so that it was now really a seven-iron. Watson had gone ahead with a birdie at the tenth, and when Seve missed from four feet for his birdie at the twelfth it seemed that his chance might be slipping away. But Watson at that same hole produced the first of two destructive shots on the inward half, a drive into the bushes forcing a penalty drop and an eventual five. There was magnificent cut-and-thrust from there until the unforgettable closing holes: a beautiful pitch to six yards at the fourteenth gained a birdie for Seve, just as Watson was making a fine three from five yards at the thirteenth. Seve at this point was wearing a white shirt and navy

Tom Watson in characteristically attacking form. *Evening Telegraph*, Dundee.

Tom Watson with caddie Alfie Fyles. Watson was paired with Ian Baker-Finch in the final round (Ballesteros and Langer were paired ahead of them). On the 1st tee Watson appeared the more nervous. To his caddie he quipped: 'Why are you shaking, Alfie?'

trousers; but on the fifteenth tee as a cooling breeze arose, he donned a navy blue sweater, just as he had worn at Lytham in 1979, and when winning the 1983 U.S. Masters. On occasion he has been known to dress in this way if he feels he has a chance of winning. Both he and Watson parred the fifteenth and sixteenth, Seve's putt for a birdie at the latter stopping on the very lip of the hole. So they were level.

On the seventeenth tee neither can have been bursting with confidence, each being level fives so far for that hole. From my vantage point behind the wall at the seventeenth I could see Ballesteros walk well left to his ball in the rough – this time in a better lie than in the earlier rounds but still about 200 yards from the pin. As he said later, his six-iron normally went 165 yards, but, suspecting a flier, he played a high, handsome shot which pitched on the front edge and ran up the bank to perhaps five yards from the drop to the dreaded road. From there he was stone-dead for the four he had promised he would achieve before the last round

The final moments and the crowd rush towards the 18th green. Police dash to get ropes in front of them. *Dundee Courier.*

Ballesteros has left the 18th green, having holed a curly 5-yarder for his 3. Watson has played his pitching wedge right on line but past the pin. In his usual sporting manner, he emerges smiling in defeat from the crowd to make his way to the 18th green. *Evening Telegraph*, Dundee.

Seve Ballesteros, British Open Golf Champion 1984, poses with the Golf Champion Trophy in St. Andrews' incomparable setting. *Dundee Courier.*

began. Watson was well right from the seventeenth tee, so far right that he stood for some time uncertain whether the ball had stayed in bounds, spread out his arms, palms up, and waited for some official down the fairway to give him the word. Not only was it in bounds, but in the perfect spot on the right side of the fairway. If anything, he was nearer the green than Seve had been. Watson decided to play a right-to-left shot with either a two-iron or a three-iron into the wind which was blowing from the left and slightly against him. As he squared up to the shot a mighty roar from the eighteenth indicated that Seve had placed his second shot some five yards from the pin. Watson walked away from his ball and then settled to the shot again. He pushed his chosen two-iron badly, thus harnessing the wind instead of fighting it: his ball bounced on the road, failed to ricochet from the wall and settled in a little rut only two feet from it. From there it would have taken a miraculous shot to get close, and with a short, stabbing seven-iron he did well to get within ten yards. At about the same time there was an extended roar from the eighteenth: Ballesteros had holed his birdie putt, the ball tumbling in the sidedoor at its very last gasp. Watson's putt, though good, was never in, and suddenly he needed a two to tie. He hit a very fine drive, and was left with a shot, by his own measurement, of ninety-three yards to the flag; with his pitching wedge he was right on line but well beyond the pin. From the moment that he had left the last tee he behaved as everyone knew he would: his smile was cheerful as the crowd applauded him; it was still there as he advanced to the green to get down in two putts; and after Baker-Finch had putted out he warmly congratulated Ballesteros on his great finish and fine victory. Certainly no worthier champion has ever crossed the Swilcan Burn and walked up that eighteenth fairway.

The Trevino Connection, the film that was being made at the time of that 1984 Championship and afterwards, was conducted through the dismantling of all these tents, scoreboards and grandstands; and when we were filming on the balcony of the Clubhouse, I found I was sitting knee to knee with Trevino while he interviewed me. But there were so many interruptions: the clapperboards would come together with a clang again and again and a voice would say 'Trevino Connection, take four (or take five), action!' At one point I heard the cameraman say, 'Hell, it's a helicopter', and so it was. While this was darting around I found I had time to have a word with Trevino and I told him that just the year before I had been playing in a four-ball on the Old Course with Hugh Campbell, a very fine Scottish international player, and that, at the long 14th with the wind very strong from left to right, I had hit a drive out over the Beardies Bunkers to the left and back onto the middle of the fairway. I was delighted to hear Campbell say, 'There was a touch of the Trevinos about that!' At this the great man gave a chuckle and a smile, and me a great rap on the knee. For this and for many other very welcome moments over the last few years I am greatly indebted to the Royal & Ancient Golf Club of St. Andrews.

POSTSCRIPT

*L*OOKING TO THE FUTURE, it is a thousand pities that Prestwick where it all began has little chance of staging a modern Open Championship. From as early as 1903 it had been clear that the layout of the course made stewarding extremely difficult, if not impossible. In 1925 the huge crowds had imposed enormous pressure on poor Macdonald Smith. He could not see the result of his longer shots, and had no peace and quiet in which to think out the best way of achieving a respectable final round. A 79 would have earned him a play-off with Jim Barnes, a score bettered by every one of the other first dozen in the final order – but he had a nightmare 82. So 1925 saw the twenty-fourth and probably the last Championship at Prestwick. St. Andrews equalled that proud total in July 1990, having seen three truly great golfers of all time notch up a second successive victory there: John Henry Taylor, James Braid, and Jack William Nicklaus.

THE ST. ANDREWS OPENS

TABLES OF RESULTS: 1873-1984
(Depending on ties, about the first dozen in each case)

1873

1	Tom Kidd, St. Andrews	91	88	179
2	Jamie Anderson, St. Andrews	91	89	180
3	Tom Morris Jnr, St. Andrews	94	89	183
3	Bob Kirk, Blackheath	91	92	183
5	Davie Strath, St. Andrews	97	90	187
6	Walter Gourlay, St. Andrews	92	96	188
7	Tom Morris Snr, St. Andrews	93	96	189
8	Mr H.A. Lamb, Blackheath	96	96	192
9	Bob Martin, St. Andrews	97	97	194
9	Willie Fernie, St. Andrews	101	93	194
11	Mr R. Armit, St. Andrews	96	99	195
11	Jas Fenton ('Skipper'), St. Andrews	94	101	195
11	J.O.F. Morris, St. Andrews	96	99	195

1876

1	Bob Martin, St. Andrews	86	90	176
1	Davie Strath, North Berwick	86	90	176
	Strath conceded a walkover			
3	Willie Park Snr, Musselburgh	94	89	183
4	Tom Morris, St. Andrews	90	95	185
4	Willie Thompson, Elie	90	95	185
4	Mungo Park, Musselburgh	95	90	185
7	Mr H. Lamb, London	94	92	186
8	Walter Gourlay, St. Andrews	98	89	187
8	George Paxton, Musselburgh	95	92	187
8	Bob Kirk, St. Andrews	95	92	187
11	Bob Kinsman, St. Andrews	88	100	188
12	Mr D. Lamb, London	95	94	189
12	Jamie Anderson, St. Andrews	96	93	189

1879

1	Jamie Anderson, St. Andrews	84	85	169
2	Andrew Kirkaldy, St. Andrews	86	86	172
3	Jamie Allan, Westward Ho!	88	84	172
	(Kirkaldy won the play-off by a shot)			
4	George Paxton, Musselburgh	89	85	174
5	Tom Kidd, St. Andrews	87	88	175
6	Bob Ferguson, Musselburgh	89	87	176

7	D. Anderson, St. Andrews	94	84	178
8	Walter Gourlay, St. Andrews	92	87	179
9	J.O.F. Morris, St. Andrews	92	87	179
10	Tom Dunn, Wimbledon	90	89	179
	(after a play-off)			
11	Mr A.W. Smith, Glasgow	90	90	180
12	J. Rennie, St. Andrews	93	88	181
12	Willie Fernie, St. Andrews	93	88	181
12	Jack Kirkaldy, St. Andrews	92	89	181

1882

1	Bob Ferguson, Musselburgh	83	88	171
2	Willie Fernie, Dumfries	88	86	174
3	Jamie Anderson, St. Andrews	87	88	175
3	Jack Kirkaldy, St. Andrews	86	89	175
3	Bob Martin, St. Andrews	89	86	175
3	Mr Fitz Boothby, St. Andrews	86	89	175
7	James Rennie, St. Andrews	90	88	178
7	Willie Park Snr, Musselburgh	89	89	178
7	Mr J. Mansfield, Edinburgh	91	87	178
7	Davie Ayton, St. Andrews	90	88	178
11	Tom Kidd, St. Andrews	87	93	180
11	Mr H. Lamb, London	88	92	180

1885

1	Bob Martin, St. Andrews	84	87	171
2	Archie Simpson, Carnoustie	83	89	172
3	Davie Ayton, St. Andrews	89	84	173
4	Willie Fernie, Felixstowe	89	85	174
5	Willie Park Jnr, Musselburgh	86	88	174
6	Bob Simpson, Carnoustie	85	89	174
	(after a play-off)			
7	Jack Burns, St. Andrews	88	87	175
8	Peter Paxton, Malvern	85	91	176
9	Willie Campbell, Musselburgh	86	91	177
9	J.O.F. Morris, St. Andrews	91	86	177
11	Mr H. Hutchinson, Westward Ho!	87	91	178
11	Jack Kirkaldy, St. Andrews	94	84	178

1880

1	Jack Burns, Warwick	86	85	171
2	Ben Sayers, North Berwick	85	87	172
3	D. Anderson Jnr, St. Andrews	86	86	172
	(after a play-off)			
4	Willie Campbell, Prestwick	84	90	174
5	Mr Leslie Balfour, Edinburgh	86	89	175
	(Later, Balfour-Melville)			
6	Andrew Kirkaldy, St. Andrews	87	89	176
6	Davie Grant, North Berwick	88	88	176
8	Sandy Herd, St. Andrews	93	84	177
9	Davie Ayton, St. Andrews	87	91	178
10	Mr J.E. Laidlay, Edinburgh	93	87	180
11	Willie Park Jnr, Musselburgh	90	92	182
11	Hugh Kirkaldy, St. Andrews	98	84	182
11	Mr H.S.C. Everard, St. Andrews	93	89	182

1891

1	Hugh Kirkaldy, St. Andrews	83	83	166
2	Andrew Kirkaldy, St. Andrews	84	84	168
3	Willie Fernie, Troon	84	84	168
	(after a play-off)			
4	Mr S. Mure Fergusson, R&A	86	84	170
5	W.D. Moore, Chester	84	87	171
6	Willie Park Jnr, Musselburgh	88	85	173
7	David Brown, Malvern	88	86	174
8	Willie Auchterlonie, St. Andrews	85	90	175
8	Mr H.H. Hilton, Royal Liverpool	85	90	175
10	Ben Sayers, North Berwick	91	85	176
10	Tom Vardon, St. Anne's on Sea	89	87	176
12	Mr John Ball Jnr, R. Liverpool	94	83	177
12	Archie Simpson, Carnoustie	86	91	177

1895

1	J.H. Taylor, Winchester	86	78	80	78	322
2	Sandy Herd, Huddersfield	82	77	82	85	326
3	Andrew Kirkaldy, St. Andrews	81	83	84	84	332
4	G. Pulford, Hoylake	84	81	83	87	335
5	Archie Simpson, Aberdeen	88	85	78	85	336
6	D. Brown, Malvern	81	89	83	84	337
6	W. Fernie, Troon	86	79	86	86	337
6	D. Anderson Jnr, St. Andrews	86	83	84	84	337
9	Ben Sayers, North Berwick	84	87	85	82	338
9	A. Toogood, Minchinhampton	85	84	83	86	338
9	H. Vardon, Bury	80	85	85	88	338
9	T. Vardon, Ilkley	82	83	84	89	338
13	Mr James Robb, St. Andrews	89	88	81	82	340

13	Mr L. Auchterlonie, St. Andrews	84	84	85	87	340

1900

1	J.H. Taylor, Richmond	79	77	78	75	309
2	Harry Vardon, Ganton	79	81	80	77	317
3	James Braid, Romford	82	81	80	79	322
4	Jack White, Seaford	80	81	82	80	323
5	Willie Auchterlonie, St. Andrews	81	85	80	80	326
6	Willie Park Jnr, Musselburgh	80	83	81	84	328
7	Mr R. Maxwell, Tantallon	81	81	86	81	329
7	Archie Simpson, Aberdeen	82	85	83	79	329
9	Ben Sayers, North Berwick	81	83	85	81	330
10	Sandy Herd, Huddersfield	81	85	81	84	331
10	Tom Vardon, Ilkley	79	87	84	81	331
10	Andrew Kirkaldy, St. Andrews	87	83	82	79	331
13	Ted Ray, Churston	88	80	85	81	334

1905

1	James Braid, Walton Heath	81	78	78	81	318
2	Rowland Jones, Wimbledon Park	81	77	87	78	323
2	J.H. Taylor, Mid-Surrey	80	85	78	80	323
4	James Kinnell, Purley Downs	82	79	82	81	324
5	Ernest Gray, Littlehampton	82	81	84	78	325
5	Arnaud Massy, North Berwick	81	80	82	82	325
7	R. Thomson, Romford	81	81	82	83	327
8	J. Sherlock, Oxford	81	84	80	83	328
9	Tom Simpson, St. Anne's	82	88	78	81	329
9	Harry Vardon, South Herts	80	82	84	83	329
11	J. Rowe, R. Ashdown Forest	87	81	80	82	330
11	Ted Ray, Ganton	85	82	81	82	330

1910

1	James Braid, Walton Heath	76	73	74	76	299
2	Sandy Herd, Huddersfield	78	74	75	76	303
3	George Duncan, Hanger Hill	73	77	71	83	304
4	L. Ayton, Bishop's Stortford	78	76	75	77	306
5	Ted Ray, Ganton	76	77	74	81	308
5	Willie Smith, Mexico	77	71	80	80	308
5	Fred Robson, West Surrey	75	80	77	76	308
8	J. Kinnell, Purley Downs	79	74	77	79	309

8	T.G. Renouf, Manchester	77	76	75	81	309
8	E.P. Gaudin, Worplesdon	78	74	76	81	309
8	D.J. Ross, Oakley County, USA	78	79	75	77	309
12	Tom Ball, Bramshot	81	77	75	78	311
12	P.J. Gaudin, Fulwell	80	79	74	78	311

1921

1	Jock Hutchison, Glenview, USA	72	75	79	70	296
2	Mr R.H. Wethered, R & A	78	75	72	71	296
	Play-off – Hutchison			74	76	150
	Wethered			77	82	159
3	Tom Kerrigan, USA	74	80	72	72	298
4	A.G. Havers, W. Lancashire	76	74	77	72	299
5	George Duncan, Hanger Hill	74	75	78	74	301
6	F. Leach, Northwood	78	75	76	73	302
6	Walter Hagen, USA	74	79	72	77	302
6	Joe Kirkwood, Australia	76	74	73	79	302
6	A. Massy, La Nivelle	74	75	74	79	302
6	Sandy Herd, Coombe Hill	74	75	74	79	302
6	Jim Barnes, USA	74	74	74	80	302
6	T. Williamson, Notts	79	71	74	78	302
13	Alec Mitchell, N. Foreland	76	79	76	71	304
13	W. Pursey, E. Devon	74	82	74	74	304

1927

1	Mr R.T. Jones, Atlanta, USA	68	72	73	72	285
2	Aubrey Boomer, St. Cloud, France	76	70	73	72	291
2	Fred Robson, Cooden Beach	76	72	69	74	291
4	E.R. Whitcombe, Bournemouth	74	73	73	73	293
4	Joe Kirkwood, USA	72	72	75	74	293
6	C.A. Whitcombe, Crews Hill	74	76	71	75	296
7	A.G. Havers, Coombe Hill	80	74	73	70	297
7	Bert Hodson, Newport, Mon.	72	70	81	74	297
9	Henry Cotton, Langley Park	73	72	77	76	298
10	Sandy Herd, Moor Park	76	75	78	71	300
10	Tom Williamson, Notts	75	76	78	71	300
10	R. Vickers, Heswell	75	75	77	73	300
10	Mr W.B. Torrance, R. Burgess	72	80	74	74	300

10	Mr T.P. Perkins, Castle Bromwich	76	78	70	76	300
10	P.H. Rodgers, St. Anne's	76	73	74	77	300
10	Percy Alliss, Germany	73	74	73	80	300

1933

1	Densmore Shute, USA	73	73	73	73	292
2	Craig Wood, USA	77	72	68	75	292
	Play-off – Shute			75	74	149
	Wood			78	76	154
3	Gene Sarazen, USA	72	73	73	75	293
3	Leo Diegel, USA	75	70	71	77	293
3	Syd Easterbrook, Knowle	73	72	71	77	293
6	Olin Dutra, USA	76	76	70	72	294
7	Reg Whitcombe, Parkstone	76	75	72	72	295
7	Alf Padgham, R. Ashdown Forest	74	73	74	74	295
7	Ed Dudley, USA	70	71	76	78	295
7	Henry Cotton, Belgium	73	71	72	79	295
7	Abe Mitchell, private	74	68	74	79	295
12	Archie Compston, Coombe Hill	72	74	77	73	296
12	Ernest Whitcombe, Meyrick Park	73	73	75	75	296

1939

1	Dick Burton, Sale	70	72	77	71	290
2	Johnny Bulla, Chicago, USA	77	71	71	73	292
3	J. Fallon, Huddersfield	71	73	71	79	294
3	Alf Perry, Leatherhead	71	74	73	76	294
3	Bill Shankland, Temple Newsam	72	73	72	77	294
3	Reg Whitcombe, Parkstone	71	75	74	74	294
3	Sam King, Knole Park	74	72	75	73	294
8	Martin Pose, Argentina	71	72	76	76	295
9	Percy Alliss, Ferndown	75	73	74	74	296
9	Ernest Kenyon, Beaconsfield	73	75	74	74	296
9	Bobby Locke, South Africa	70	75	76	75	296
12	Dai Rees, Hindhead	71	74	75	77	297
13	James Adams, R. Liverpool	73	74	75	76	298
13	Henry Cotton, Ashridge	74	72	76	76	298
13	Mr Jimmy Bruen, Cork	72	75	75	76	298
13	E. Bertolino, Argentina	73	75	75	75	298

1946

1	Sam Snead, USA	71	70	74	75	290
2	Bobby Locke, South Africa	69	74	75	76	294
2	Johnny Bulla, USA	71	72	72	79	294
4	Charlie Ward, Little Aston	73	73	73	76	295
4	Henry Cotton, Royal Mid-Surrey	70	70	76	79	295
4	Dai Rees, Hindhead	75	67	73	80	295
4	Norman von Nida, Australia	70	76	74	75	295
8	Fred Daly, Balmoral	77	71	76	74	298
8	Joe Kirkwood, USA	71	75	78	74	298
10	Lawson Little, USA	78	75	72	74	299
11	Harry Bradshaw, Kilcroney	76	75	76	73	300
12	Dick Burton, Sale	74	76	76	76	302
13	Bill Shankland, Templenewsam	76	76	77	75	304
14	Reg Whitcombe, Parkstone	71	76	82	76	305
14	W. Anderson, Murcar	76	76	78	75	305

1955

1	Peter Thomson, Australia	71	68	70	72	281
2	John Fallon, Huddersfield	73	67	73	70	283
3	Frank Jowle, Edgbaston	70	71	69	74	284
4	Bobby Locke, South Africa	74	69	70	72	285
5	A. Cerda, Argentina	73	71	71	71	286
5	Ken Bousfield, Coombe Hill	71	75	70	70	286
5	Harry Weetman, Croham Hurst	71	71	70	74	286
5	Bernard Hunt, Hartsbourne	70	71	74	71	286
5	Flory van Donck, Belgium	71	72	71	72	286
10	R. Barbieri, Argentina	71	71	73	72	287
10	Christie O'Connor, Bundoran	71	75	70	71	287
12	Eric Brown, Buchanan Castle	69	70	73	76	288
12	Fred Daly, Balmoral	75	72	70	71	288
12	John Jacobs, Sandy Lodge	71	70	71	76	288

1957

1	Bobby Locke, South Africa	69	72	68	70	279
2	Peter Thomson, Australia	73	69	70	70	282
3	Eric Brown, Buchanan Castle	67	72	73	71	283
4	A. Miguel, Spain	72	72	69	72	285
5	David Thomas, Sudbury	72	74	70	70	286
5	Tom Haliburton, Wentworth	72	73	68	73	286
5	Mr W.D. Smith, Prestwick	71	72	72	71	286

5	Flory van Donck, Belgium	72	68	74	72	286
9	Henry Cotton, Temple	74	72	69	72	287
9	Max Faulkner, Selsey	74	70	71	72	287
9	A. Cerda, Argentina	71	71	72	73	287
12	Peter Alliss, Parkstone	72	74	74	68	288
12	Harry Weetman, Croham Hurst	75	71	71	71	288
14	Cary Middlecoff, USA	72	71	74	72	289

1960

1	Kel Nagle, Australia	69	67	71	71	278
2	Arnold Palmer, USA	70	71	70	68	279
3	Bernard Hunt, Hartsbourne	72	73	71	66	282
3	Harold Henning, South Africa	72	72	69	69	282
3	Roberto de Vicenzo, Mexico	67	67	75	73	282
6	Mr Guy Wolstenholme, Sunningdale	74	70	71	68	283
7	Gary Player, South Africa	72	71	72	69	284
8	Mr J.B. Carr, Sutton	72	73	67	73	285
9	Harry Weetman, Selsdon Park	74	70	71	71	286
9	Syd Scott, Roehampton	73	71	67	75	286
9	Dai Rees, South Herts	73	71	73	69	286
9	Major D.A. Blair, R&A	70	73	71	72	286
9	Eric Brown, Buchanan Castle	75	68	72	71	286
9	Peter Thomson, Australia	72	69	75	70	286

1964

1	Tony Lema, USA	73	68	68	70	279
2	Jack Nicklaus, USA	76	74	66	68	284
3	Roberto de Vicenzo, Argentina	76	72	70	67	285
4	Bernard Hunt, Hartsbourne	73	74	70	70	287
5	Bruce Devlin, Australia	72	72	73	73	290
6	Christie O'Connor, R. Dublin	71	73	74	73	291
6	Harry Weetman, Selsdon Park	72	71	75	73	291
8	Gary Player, South Africa	78	71	73	70	292
8	Harold Henning, South Africa	78	73	71	70	292
8	A. Miguel, Spain	73	76	72	71	292
11	Doug Sanders, USA	78	73	74	68	293
12	Frank Phillips, Australia	77	75	72	70	294
13	David Thomas, Sunningdale	75	74	75	72	296
13	C. Greene, Milltown	74	76	73	73	296

13	R.L. Moffitt,					
	Coventry Hearsall	76	72	74	74	296
13	J. Garaialde, France	71	74	79	72	296

1970

1	Jack Nicklaus, USA	68	69	73	73	283
2	Doug Sanders, USA	68	71	71	73	283
	Play-off – Nicklaus					72
	Sanders					73
3	Harold Henning,					
	South Africa	67	72	73	73	285
3	Lee Trevino, USA	68	68	72	77	285
5	Tony Jacklin, Potters Bar	67	70	73	76	286
6	Peter Oosterhuis,					
	Dulwich & Sydenham	73	69	69	76	287
6	Neil Coles, Coombe Hill	65	74	72	76	287
8	H. Jackson, Knockbracken	69	72	73	74	288
9	John Panton, Glenbervie	72	73	73	71	289
9	Peter Thomson, Australia	68	74	73	74	289
9	Tommy Horton,					
	Ham Manor	66	73	75	75	289
12	Arnold Palmer, USA	68	72	76	74	290

1978

1	Jack Nicklaus, USA	71	72	69	69	281
2	Simon Owen,					
	New Zealand	70	75	67	71	283

2	Raymond Floyd, USA	69	75	71	68	283
2	Ben Crenshaw, USA	70	69	73	71	283
2	Tom Kite, USA	72	69	72	70	283
6	Peter Oosterhuis,					
	Great Britain	72	70	69	73	284
7	Isao Aoki, Japan	68	71	73	73	285
7	Bob Shearer, Australia	71	69	74	71	285
7	John Schroeder, USA	74	69	70	72	285
7	Nick Faldo, unattached	71	72	70	72	285
11	Orville Moody, USA	73	69	74	70	286
11	Michael Cahill, Australia	71	72	75	68	286
11	Dale Hayes, South Africa	74	70	71	71	286

1984

1	Seve Ballesteros, Spain	69	68	70	69	276
2	Bernhard Langer,					
	W. Germany	71	68	68	71	278
2	Tom Watson, USA	71	68	66	73	278
4	Fred Couples, USA	70	69	74	68	281
4	Lanny Wadkins, USA	70	69	73	69	281
6	Greg Norman, Australia	67	74	74	67	282
7	Mark McCumber, USA	74	67	72	70	283
8	Graham Marsh, Australia	70	74	73	67	284
8	Sam Torrance,					
	Great Britain	74	74	66	70	284
8	Ronan Rafferty, Ireland	74	72	67	71	284
8	Hugh Baiocchi, S. Africa	72	70	70	72	284
8	Ian Baker-Finch, Australia	68	66	71	79	284

Dates of, and Prize-money at, the St. Andrews Opens

1873	4th October:	Winner £11, 'and four prizes from £7 downwards'
1876	7th October:	Winner £10, second (Strath) £5, and six totalling £12
1879	4th October:	Winner £10, second £7, and prizes totalling £29
1882	30th September:	Winner £12, second £9, and other unspecified prizes
1885	3rd October:	Winner £10, second £7, and seven prizes totalling £18
1888	6th October:	Winner £8, second £6, and four prizes totalling £6
1891	6th October:	Winner £10, second £6, and five prizes totalling £12 10/-
1895[1]	12th-13th June:	Winner £30, second £20, third £10; total prizes £90.
1900	6th-7th June:	Winner £50, second £25, third £15; total prizes £115
1905[2]	9th-11th June:	Winner £50, second equal £20; only six prizes totalling £115
1910	22nd-25th June:	Winner £50, second £25, third £15; total prizes £125
1921	22nd-25th June:	Winner £75; total prizes £225
1927	12th-14th July:	Winner £100; total prizes £275
1933	6th-8th July:	Winner £100; total prizes £500
1939	5th-7th July:	Winner £100; total prizes £500
1946	3rd-5th July:	Winner £150; total prizes £1,000
1955	6th-8th July:	Winner £1,000; total prizes £3,750
1957	3rd-5th July:	Winner £1,000; total prizes £3,750
1960	6th-9th July:	Winner £1,250; total prizes £7,000
1964	8th-10th July:	Winner £1,500; total prizes £8,500
1970[3]	8th-12th July:	Winner £5,250; total prizes £40,000
1978	12th-15th July:	Winner £12,500; total prizes £125,000
1984[4]	19th-22nd July:	Winner £55,000; total prizes £451,000
1990	19th-22nd July:	Winner £85,000; total prizes £825,000

[1] Entrance fee of 10/- from 1893 on.
[2] 3 days from 1904 on.
[3] 4 days from 1966 on.
[4] Prize-money increased by 10% in mid-Championship.

INDEX